For

TATE + LYLE'S
RECIPES FOR YOUNG COOKS

Delicious ideas for balanced eating by

Lorna Rhodes

MARTIN BOOKS

Published by Martin Books
a division of Woodhead-Faulkner
(Publishers) Limited, Simon & Schuster
International Group, Fitzwilliam House,
32 Trumpington Street, Cambridge CB2 1QY

First published 1988 © Woodhead-Faulkner Ltd
ISBN 0 85941 456 6

Conditions of sale
All rights reserved. No part of this publication may be
reproduced, stored in a retrieval system or transmitted,
in any form or by any means, electronic, mechanical,
photocopying, recording or otherwise, without the
prior permission of the copyright owners.

Lorna Rhodes is an experienced cookery writer
and home economist who worked for several
major food companies. She is now a busy
working mother – a freelance
consultant, and contributor
to numerous magazines.

Design: by Design, Newmarket
Colour illustrations: Mandy Doyle
Line illustrations: Richard Jacobs
Typesetting: Goodfellow & Egan, Cambridge
Printed and bound in
Singapore by Toppan

Contents

INTRODUCTION
page 4

SUPPERS, SNACKS AND SAVOURIES
page 8

TASTY BAKES
page 26

DELICIOUS DESSERTS
page 42

SPECIAL OCCASIONS
page 56

TO MAKE AND GIVE
page 70

INDEX
page 80

INTRODUCTION

Most of us enjoy cooking because there is something tasty to eat at the end. Here is a Cookery Book to give you lots of ideas, both sweet and savoury, to try at home or at school.

It is important that we eat to stay fit and healthy, and also that we enjoy our food. Our bodies need several different kinds of food, containing the necessary nutrients, and we should try to eat the right quantities of all of them: we should have a 'balanced diet'. Our meal-times should be regular, and should be something to look forward to. If meals are appetising, there is less temptation to eat too many snacks in-between.

Also, remember that your teeth are very important and must be cleaned regularly, to make sure that nothing is left in your mouth to cause decay.

HINTS AND TIPS

Standard spoon measurements are used in all recipes:
1 tablespoon = one 15 ml spoon
1 teaspoon = one 5 ml spoon
All spoon measures are level.
All eggs are standard size 3, i.e. medium.
– When using the recipes in this book, follow the measurements from one column only and keep to it – do not mix the two columns, as one is metric and the other imperial. Here is an example:

CUCUMBER DIP

Metric		Imperial
½	cucumber	½
5 ml	salt	1 teaspoon
250 g	thick Greek yogurt	8 oz
5 ml	fresh chopped mint	1 teaspoon
	fresh ground pepper	

THE USE OF THE DIFFERENT FOOD NUTRIENTS

Protein
In foods like: meat, poultry, fish, eggs, milk, cheese, nuts, beans, peas, yeast.

This is *very* important for growing, and gives us strong bones and bodies.

Carbohydrates
Starches
In foods like: bread, pasta, rice, flour, breakfast cereals, potatoes.
Sugars
In foods like: sugar itself, syrup, honey.

These give us lots of readily available energy.

Fats
In foods like: butter, margarine, milk, cheese, nuts, meat.

These provide energy reserves for building and replacing body tissues.

Fibre
In foods like: fruit and vegetables and their skins, peas, beans, nuts, lentils, dried fruit, bread, wholemeal foods.

All these foods are very good for our digestion.

Vitamins and minerals
These are found in lots of foods, and they all help us in different ways. There are *vitamins* in fruit, vegetables, eggs, milk, cheese, bread, yeast, nuts and fish, and a number of other foods. *Minerals* include calcium, which helps with growing bones and healthy teeth, and iron, which helps our blood and nervous system.

Introduction

You will notice the wide variety of sugars used in this book, each chosen because it is the most suitable for the recipe:

Granulated sugar is used for general sweetening purposes.

Caster sugar has a finer grain than granulated, so is more suitable for baking.

Light-brown soft sugar is fine-grained, creamy gold in colour, and has a mild syrup flavour – use it for baking too.

Demerara sugar has a golden colour and delicate syrup flavour. It has larger crystals than the soft sugar so it is ideal for giving a crunchy topping to cakes and biscuits.

Dark-brown soft sugar not only sweetens, but also also adds colour, and gives a distinctive flavour to any recipe. It is ideal for rich cakes, puddings and mincemeat.

Icing sugar is very fine in texture and is ideal for decorating cakes and making sweets.

Lyle's golden syrup is also used to give its own special flavour to many baking recipes in this book.

Measuring Lyle's golden syrup:
When using a tablespoon, rinse the spoon in very hot water before use, then the syrup can slide off easily without waste.
When measuring syrup before melting it, weigh the saucepan, and then carefully spoon the syrup into the pan on the scales until you have the required amount.

If you would like any more information about sugar, please write to:
   The Home Economist
   Tate and Lyle Sugars
   Enterprise House
   45 Homesdale Road
   Bromley BR2 9TE

I am sure you will now have lots of fun making these recipes and letting your family and friends sample the delicious results.

Before you start cooking here are a few things you must do:
- For younger children, make sure that there is an adult to help you or, if you are older, ask permission to use the kitchen.
- Before handling food, always wash your hands, and put on an apron.
- Read through the recipe and make sure that you have everything you need, then collect all the ingredients together.
- When using the recipes in this book, follow the measurements from one column only and keep to it – do not mix the two columns, as one is metric and the other imperial.
- If using the oven, make sure the shelves are in the right position; cook things on the middle shelf unless the recipe says otherwise.
- Always use a wooden chopping board for cutting.
- Use small knives as they are easier to handle; and when chopping, keep your fingers away from the blade.
- When using saucepans, turn the handles away from the edge of the stove so that you do not knock them over.

Always turn the saucepan handle away from the edge of the stove

Introduction

- If boiling anything, especially sugar or syrup, be extra careful, as the liquid will be very hot.
- When transferring hot pans or dishes from the stove or oven, make a space ready for them first, and place them on a wooden board or mat.
- Always use oven-gloves before picking up anything hot and taking things out of the oven.
- Never use an electric mixer, blender or food processor unless an adult is helping.
- If you spill anything on the floor, wipe it up at once so that no one will slip.
- When you have finished cooking, make sure the oven is turned off.
- Last but not least, wash all the utensils you have used.

EQUIPMENT YOU WILL NEED

Scales – these are used for measuring dry and solid ingredients before you start cooking.

Measuring jug – this is used to measure liquid ingredients, unless the amount is very small.

Measuring spoons – these are used to measure small quantities of dry and wet ingredients. When measuring out dry ingredients, make sure that they are level with the edge of the spoon unless the recipe says rounded, when the food is heaped above the edge of the spoon.

Mixing bowls – different sizes are used depending on the amount of mixture to be made.

Rolling pin – this is used to roll out pastry and doughs. Always dust with flour before using.

Wooden spoons – these are used for mixing, and for stirring mixtures cooking in saucepans.

Whisk – this can be a wire balloon whisk, a rotary whisk or a hand-held electric whisk.

Grater – this is used to grate the rinds from fruit, or to grate cheese.

Lemon squeezer – this is used to extract the juice from lemons and oranges.

Pastry cutters – these are used to cut out biscuits and scones; you may need fancy shapes for some recipes.

Pastry brush – this is helpful for coating or glazing food evenly with milk, water, egg or oil.

Sieve – this is a mesh through which you can shake flour or icing sugar to get rid of any lumps.

Palette knife – this is useful for lifting food from one place to another. You can also use a fish slice.

Baking trays – these are large flat metal trays used to bake a number of items, such as biscuits, in the oven.

Baking tins – these can be all sorts of shapes and sizes; the recipe will tell you which one you need.

Wire cooling rack – cooked food is placed on this to help it cool down quickly, as the air can circulate through the mesh.

Spatula – this is used to scrape out the bowl so that you do not leave any mixture behind.

Introduction

COOKING WORDS USED IN THIS BOOK

Bake – to cook food in the oven.

Beat – to mix food with a wooden spoon or hand-held electric whisk to make the food light and fluffy.

Boil – to heat a liquid until the surface bubbles.

Breadcrumbs – you can make these either by putting bread in an electric blender or food processor to reduce it to crumbs, or by grating bread on the coarse side of a grater.

Chill – to cool food in the refrigerator.

Chop – to cut food into smaller pieces with a sharp knife. Use a wooden board.

Fold in – to mix the ingredients in with each other gently, using a metal spoon.

Folding in

Fry – to cook in hot fat or oil.

Glaze – to brush food with beaten egg or milk to give it a glossy finish.

Grease – to brush the inside of a dish or baking tin with oil, margarine or butter, to stop food sticking.

Grill – to cook food under the grill.

Knead – to work a dough with your hands until the surface is smooth.

Marinate – to soak meat or chicken in a mixture which gives it flavour – the mixture is called a *marinade*.

Rub in – to mix ingredients together with your fingertips until the mixture looks like breadcrumbs.

Rubbing in

Season – to add enough salt and pepper to a dish to give it flavour.

Simmer – to cook food over a low heat, after bringing it to the boil, so that it *just* bubbles.

SUPPERS, SNACKS AND SAVOURIES

CUCUMBER DIP

Ingredients – serves 6–8

½	cucumber	½
5 ml	salt	I teaspoon
250 g	thick Greek yogurt	8 oz
5 ml	chopped fresh mint	I teaspoon
	freshly ground pepper	

Equipment you will need:
Chopping board, knife, colander, kitchen paper, medium bowl, spoon.

This cool cucumber dip can be served as a starter or as part of a picnic or barbecue meal. Scoop up the dip with pieces of warm pitta bread, or dip in sticks of celery and carrot.

This is what you do:

1 Cut the cucumber in very small pieces, put into the colander and sprinkle over the salt. Mix in the salt then stand on the draining board for 30 minutes.
2 Rinse the cucumber, and turn it onto a double thickness of kitchen paper to allow the moisture to be absorbed.
3 Tip the cucumber into the bowl, stir in the yogurt and mint and season with pepper. Mix well, then serve.

SARDINE PUFFS

Ingredients – makes 10

125 g	can sardines in tomato sauce	4 oz
25 g	fresh breadcrumbs	I oz
30 ml	single cream or natural yogurt	2 tablespoons
200 g	frozen puff pastry, thawed	7 oz
	flour for rolling	
	milk to glaze	

Equipment you will need:
Baking tray, can opener, medium bowl, fork, rolling pin, pastry brush, knife.

These make a change from sausage rolls and can be served as a snack or a light lunch with salad.

This is what you do:

1 Heat the oven to Gas Mark 7/220°C/425°F. Grease the baking tray.
2 Open the can of sardines and turn into a bowl with the sauce. Mash with a fork then stir in the breadcrumbs and cream or yogurt.
3 Roll out the pastry on a floured surface to make a long rectangle about 40 × 13 cm (15 × 5 inches).
4 Spread the sardine mixture over half of the pastry all along its length. Dampen the edges with water then roll up like a swiss roll, starting from the long side.
5 Cut the roll into 10 pieces, place them cut-side down on the baking tray and brush with a little milk. Bake in the oven for 12–15 minutes or until puffed up and golden. Remove from the oven, turn off the heat and serve while hot.

Cucumber Dip, Sardine Puffs and Stuffed Tomatoes

Suppers, Snacks and Savouries

	Ingredients – serves 4	
4	large tomatoes	4
1	small onion	1
75 g	back bacon	3 oz
15 g	butter	½ oz
25 g	wholemeal breadcrumbs	1 oz
50 g	Cheddar cheese	2 oz
	pinch dried mixed herbs	
	salt and freshly ground pepper	

Equipment you will need:
Chopping board, knife with serrated edge, teaspoon, small frying pan or saucepan, wooden spoon, bowl, grater, ovenproof dish.

STUFFED TOMATOES

These savoury tomatoes make a tasty lunch. Serve with a mixed salad and crusty bread.

This is what you do:

1. Heat the oven to Gas Mark 4/180°C/350°F.
2. Cut the tops off the tomatoes. With the point of the serrated knife, cut round the inside. Using the teaspoon, scoop out the pulp of the tomatoes (this can be used later in a soup or sauce recipe).
3. Skin the onion and chop very finely. Chop the bacon into small pieces. Put the butter in the pan, place on the stove and melt over a medium heat. Add the onion and bacon and cook for 5 minutes, stirring with the wooden spoon. Turn off the heat.
4. Tip the onion and bacon mixture into the bowl and stir in the breadcrumbs.
5. Coarsely grate the cheese then add it to the bowl. Stir in the herbs and season with salt and pepper.
6. Divide the filling between the tomatoes, pressing it well inside each tomato. Place in an ovenproof dish. Put the tops back on the tomatoes, then cook in the oven for 15–20 minutes. Remove from the oven, turn off the heat and serve while hot.

Suppers, Snacks and Savouries

SWEET AND SOUR PORK

Ingredients — serves 4

500 g	pork leg steaks or pork fillet	1 lb
1	small onion	1
1	green pepper	1
125 g	button mushrooms	4 oz
30 ml	sunflower oil	2 tablespoons
300 ml	pineapple and/or orange juice	½ pint
30 ml	Lyle's golden syrup	2 tablespoons
45 ml	cider vinegar	3 tablespoons
30 ml	light soy sauce	2 tablespoons
30 ml	tomato ketchup	2 tablespoons
30 ml	cornflour	2 tablespoons

Equipment you will need:
Chopping board, knife,
large frying pan with lid,
wooden spoon, cup.

Serve this dish with some boiled rice or chinese-style egg noodles.

This is what you do:

1 Cut the pork into small cubes. Peel and chop the onion. Slice the top off the pepper, remove the core and seeds, and cut into small pieces. Wash the mushrooms and quarter them.

2 Heat the oil in the frying pan on the stove, add the pork and onion and cook, stirring, over a medium heat for about 8 minutes until the pork is lightly browned.

3 Add the pepper and mushrooms to the pan and cook for a further 3 minutes. Stir in the rest of the ingredients except the cornflour.

4 Bring to the boil then turn down the heat. Cover the pan and simmer gently for 20–25 minutes until the pork is tender.

5 Put the cornflour in the cup and blend with a little water until smooth. Remove the lid from the pan and stir in the cornflour. Continue to simmer for 2–3 minutes until the sauce thickens. Remove the pan from the stove and turn off the heat.

Suppers, Snacks and Savouries

Ingredients – serves 4

40 g	butter	1 ½ oz
4	slices softgrain bread	4
200 g	ham sausage	7 oz
6	eggs	6
45 ml	milk	3 tablespoons
	salt and freshly ground pepper	

Equipment you will need:
Medium saucepan, chopping board, knife, pastry brush, 4 yorkshire pudding tins, baking tray, small bowl, fork, wooden spoon.

HAM AND EGG TOASTIES

These toasties can also be made with cooked smoked fish or lightly cooked chopped mushrooms instead of the ham.

This is what you do:

1 Heat the oven to Gas Mark 4/180°C/350°F.
2 Put the butter into the saucepan and place on the stove over a low heat until melted. Turn off the heat.
3 Cut the crusts off the bread. Lightly brush one side of each slice with the melted butter then press a slice, buttered side down, into each yorkshire pudding tin. Lightly brush the other side of the bread with melted butter, leaving a little butter in the pan. Place the tins on a baking tray and bake in the oven for 20 minutes or until crisp and golden brown.
4 While the bread is cooking, peel the skin from the ham sausage and cut it into small pieces. Break the eggs into the bowl, add the milk, season with salt and pepper and whisk together with a fork.
5 Return the saucepan to the stove over a low heat. Pour in the egg mixture and add the ham. Stirring with a wooden spoon, cook until set but still creamy. Turn off the heat.
6 Remove the bread cases from the oven, and place them on serving plates. Divide the scrambled egg filling between them and serve at once.

Ham and Egg Toasties

Stereo

Suppers, Snacks and Savouries

Ingredients — serves 4

400 g	can peach slices	13 oz
4	small gammon slices	4
30 ml	demerara sugar	2 tablespooons

Equipment you will need:
Can opener, sieve, fish slice.

Ingredients — serves 4

For the fish fingers:

12	fish fingers	12
15 ml	oil	1 tablespoon
350 g	packet fresh stir-fry vegetables	12 oz

For the sauce:

15 ml	cornflour	1 tablespoon
250 ml	chicken stock	8 fl oz
15 ml	soy sauce	1 tablespoon
10 ml	vinegar	2 teaspoons
15 ml	light-brown soft sugar	1 tablespoon
5 ml	tomato purée	1 teaspoon
	pinch ground ginger	

Equipment you will need:
Medium saucepan, 2 wooden
spoons, fish slice or tongs,
large frying pan.

GRILLED HAM WITH PEACHES

A quick and easy meal to prepare. Serve with jacket potatoes and a green vegetable.

This is what you do:

1 Open the can of peaches and drain through the sieve (you can save the juice to make a jelly later).
2 Heat the grill to moderate, and arrange the ham steaks on the grill rack. Cook for 3–4 minutes.
3 Turn the ham steaks over and place peach slices over each; sprinkle with the sugar then return to the grill and cook for a further 3–4 minutes. Remove from the grill and turn off the heat.

ORIENTAL FISH FINGERS

Here is a new way of serving fish fingers that all the family will enjoy. Serve with boiled rice.

This is what you do:

1 To make the sauce, put the cornflour into the saucepan and gradually blend in the stock. Add the rest of the ingredients for the sauce, then put the pan on the stove. Heat, stirring with a wooden spoon, until the sauce comes to boiling point. Reduce the heat and simmer for 2 minutes. Turn off the heat.
2 For the fish fingers, heat the grill to moderate, arrange the fish fingers on the rack and grill for 8–10 minutes (turning once with a fish slice or tongs) until they are golden on both sides. Turn off the grill.
3 While the fish fingers are cooking, pour the oil into the frying pan and set on the stove over a high heat. Add the stir-fry vegetables and cook, stirring them around, for about 3–4 minutes. Take them off the heat and quickly re-heat the sauce. Turn off the heat.
4 Divide the vegetables between four plates, place the fish fingers on top then drizzle over the sauce.

Suppers, Snacks and Savouries

Ingredients – serves 4

500 g	pork sausages	1 lb
For the sauce:		
10 ml	cornflour	2 teaspoons
300 ml	water	1/2 pint
10 ml	soy sauce	2 teaspoons
10 ml	vinegar	2 teaspoons
10 ml	dark-brown soft sugar	2 teaspoons
30 ml	tomato ketchup	2 tablespoons
30 ml	tomato pickle	2 tablespoons
	salt and freshly ground pepper	

Equipment you will need:
Tongs, medium saucepan,
wooden spoon.

Ingredients – serves 6

250 g	dried haricot beans	8 oz
1	large onion	1
125 g	bacon	4 oz
15 ml	sunflower oil	1 tablespoon
300 ml	vegetable stock	1/2 pint
30 ml	tomato purée	2 tablespoons
15 ml	dark-brown soft sugar	1 tablespoon
10 ml	mustard powder	2 teaspoons
	salt and freshly ground pepper	

Equipment you will need:
Bowl, sieve, large saucepan,
1.75-litre (3-pint) casserole dish,
chopping board, knife,
wooden spoon.

SAUSAGES WITH BARBECUE SAUCE

The sauce for these sausages is also good served with beefburgers, especially if they have been cooked on a barbecue.

This is what you do:

1 Heat the grill to moderately high, place the sausages on the grill rack and grill for 10–12 minutes, turning once with the tongs. When they are cooked, turn off the grill.
2 While the sausages are cooking, make the sauce. Put the cornflour into the saucepan, gradually add the water then stir in the rest of the ingredients.
3 Put the saucepan on the stove and heat, stirring with the wooden spoon, until boiling. Reduce the heat and simmer for 2 minutes. Turn off the heat and pour into a sauceboat or jug, to serve with the sausages.

BOSTON BAKED BEANS

You will need to soak the dried beans overnight first.

This is what you do:

1 Put the beans into the bowl, cover with cold water and leave to stand overnight.
2 The next day, tip them into a sieve and drain them.
3 Put the beans into the saucepan, cover with fresh water then place on the stove and heat until boiling. Reduce the heat and simmer for 30 minutes. Turn off the heat.
4 Tip the beans into the sieve and drain again. Put into the casserole dish.
5 Heat the oven to Gas Mark 3/160°C/325°F.
6 Peel and chop the onion. Remove the rind from the bacon and chop. Put the oil in the saucepan and heat on the stove. Add the onion and bacon and cook over a low heat for 5 minutes, stirring with the wooden spoon. Turn off the heat.
7 Add, with the rest of the ingredients, to the beans. Mix well then cover the casserole and cook in the oven for about 1 hour or until the beans are tender. Remove from the oven and turn off the heat.

Suppers, Snacks and Savouries

SAUSAGE PASTA POT

Ingredients – serves 4

I	onion	I
I	red or green pepper	I
15 ml	sunflower oil	I tablespoon
500 g	thick pork sausages	I lb
400 g	can chopped tomatoes	13 oz
300 ml	chicken stock	½ pint
5 ml	dried mixed herbs	I teaspoon
125 g	pasta shapes	4 oz
	salt and freshly ground pepper	

Equipment you will need:
Chopping board, knife, large
saucepan with lid, wooden
spoon, can opener.

This is what you do:

1 Peel and chop the onion. Cut the top off the pepper, remove the core and seeds and cut into slices.
2 Pour the oil into the saucepan. Place on the stove, add the sausages and cook over a medium heat until they are lightly browned. Remove from the pan and put on a plate.
3 Add the onion to the pan and cook for 3–4 minutes, then add the pepper and cook for 2 minutes.
4 Cut the sausages in half and return to the pan.
5 Open the can of tomatoes. Stir, with the stock and herbs, into the sausage mixture, and season with salt and pepper. Bring to the boil and add the pasta.
6 Cover the pan and simmer for 15–20 minutes. Turn off the heat and serve.

TUNABURGERS

Ingredients – serves 4

2 × 200g	can tuna in brine	2 × 7 oz
4	spring onions	4
I	egg	I
75 g	wholemeal breadcrumbs	3 oz
15 ml	lemon juice	I tablespoon
15 ml	salad cream	I tablespoon
	salt and freshly ground pepper	

Equipment you will need:
Can opener, sieve, large
mixing bowl, fork, chopping
board, knife, fish slice.

This is what you do:

1 Open the can of tuna and drain through a sieve. Put into the bowl and break up the fish with a fork.
2 Chop the spring onions into very small pieces then add, with the egg, breadcrumbs, lemon juice and salad cream, to the tuna. Season with salt and pepper. Mix until well blended.
3 Divide the mixture into 8 and form into burger shapes with your hands.
4 Heat the grill to medium then arrange the tunaburgers on the grill rack. Grill for 4–5 minutes each side, or until golden, turning with the fish slice. Turn off the grill and serve.

Sausage Pasta Pot

Suppers, Snacks and Savouries

VESUVIUS SALAD

Ingredients – serves 4

	salt	
175 g	pasta	6 oz
30 ml	salad dressing (see page 24)	2 tablespoons
4	tomatoes	4
125 g	Cheddar cheese	4 oz
½	cucumber	½
1	red pepper	1
175 g	stick or piece of salami	6 oz

Equipment you will need:
Medium saucepan, colander, large, round, shallow serving dish, chopping board, knife.

This is a fun salad to make – you layer up all the ingredients, to resemble a mountain. If possible, buy different-coloured pasta in interesting shapes, such as shells or twists.

This is what you do:

1. Half-fill the saucepan with water, add a little salt then put on the stove and heat until boiling. Add the pasta and cook for about 8–10 minutes until only just tender. Turn off the heat.
2. Tip the pasta into the colander over the sink then hold under a running cold tap to rinse. Allow to drain.
3. Put the pasta into the serving dish and pour over the dressing. Toss together, then level out.
4. Chop the tomatoes, then place on top of the pasta, leaving a border of 2.5 cm (1 inch).
5. Cut the cheese into small squares and place on top of the tomatoes, leaving a 1 cm (½-inch) border.
6. Dice the cucumber and place on top of the cheese leaving a 1 cm (½-inch) border.
7. Slice the top off the pepper, remove the core and seeds, then cut the pepper into thin strips and pile on top of the salad.
8. Finally, remove the skin from the salami, cut into small pieces and scatter round the bottom of the salad on top of the pasta. The salad is now ready to serve.

Vesuvius Salad

Suppers, Snacks and Savouries

Ingredients – serves 4

For the casserole:

1	medium onion	1
15 ml	sunflower oil	1 tablespoon
500 g	lean minced beef	1 lb
250 g	can tomatoes	8 oz
30 ml	tomato purée	2 tablespoons
2.5 ml	mixed herbs	½ teaspoon
	pinch sugar	
	salt and freshly ground pepper	
175 g	wholewheat macaroni	6 oz

For the topping:

5 ml	cornflour	1 teaspoon
150 g	natural yogurt	5.3 fl oz
1	egg	1
50 g	Cheddar cheese	2 oz

Equipment you will need:
Chopping board, knife, large saucepan with lid, wooden spoon, can opener, medium saucepan, colander, 1.2-litre (2-pint) ovenproof casserole, mixing bowl, fork, grater, plate.

MACARONI MINCE LAYER

This delicious dish is a variation on spaghetti bolognese. Serve with a salad.

This is what you do:

1. Heat the oven to Gas Mark 5/190°C/375°F.
2. To make the casserole, peel the onion and chop it fairly finely. Put it into the large saucepan with the oil and minced beef and place on the stove over a medium heat. Cook, stirring with a wooden spoon, for 5 minutes, or until the onions are soft.
3. Open the can of tomatoes and tip into the pan with their juice. Stir in the tomato purée, herbs, sugar and seasoning. Bring to the boil. Cover the pan, turn the heat to low and simmer for 15 minutes. Remove from the stove and turn off the heat.
4. Half-fill the medium saucepan with water, add a little salt then bring to the boil and stir in the macaroni. Lower the heat and simmer for 10 minutes until only just tender. Remove from the stove and turn off the heat. Drain in the colander.
5. Spoon half the meat mixture into the ovenproof dish, spoon over half the macaroni then repeat.
6. To make the topping, put the cornflour into the bowl and blend in the yogurt. Add the egg and whisk with a fork.
7. Coarsely grate the cheese onto a plate and stir into the yogurt mixture. Pour evenly over the top of the macaroni. Bake in the oven for 30 minutes or until golden on top. Remove from the oven and turn off the heat.

Suppers, Snacks and Savouries

Ingredients — serves 4

For the base:

250 g	wholemeal self-raising flour, plus extra for rolling	8 oz
	pinch salt	
50 g	margarine, plus extra for greasing	2 oz
75–90 ml	milk	5–6 tablespoons

For the topping:

1	small onion	1
15 ml	sunflower oil	1 tablespoon
40 ml	tomato purée	8 teaspoons
2	large tomatoes	2
2.5 ml	dried mixed herbs	½ teaspoon
	salt and freshly ground pepper	
4	frankfurters	4
50 g	Edam or Gouda cheese	2 oz

Equipment you will need:
Baking tray, mixing bowl, spoon, rolling pin, knife, chopping board, small saucepan, wooden spoon, grater.

FRANKFURTER PIZZAS

These pizzas are quick to make, as they have a scone base. Try different toppings, such as chopped ham or sliced mushrooms and peppers.

This is what you do:

1 Heat the oven to Gas Mark 6/200°C/400°F. Grease the baking tray.

2 To make the base, put the flour into the bowl with the salt and margarine and rub together with your fingertips until the mixture looks like fine breadcrumbs.

3 Mix in the milk to make a soft dough. Turn out onto a floured work surface and divide into four. Knead each portion lightly then roll out to a thickness of about 5 mm (¼ inch). Put onto the baking tray.

4 To make the topping, peel the onion and chop. Put the oil into the saucepan, place on the stove over a medium heat, add the onion and cook for 3 minutes until tender.

5 Spread 2 teaspoonfuls of tomato purée on each scone base then divide the onion between them. Slice the tomatoes and arrange on the pizzas. Season with the mixed herbs, salt and pepper. Cut the frankfurters into chunks and put on the tomatoes.

6 Coarsely grate the cheese then scatter over the frankfurters. Cook the pizzas in the oven for 20 minutes. Remove from the oven and turn off the heat.

Suppers, Snacks and Savouries

Ingredients – serves 4–6

For the base:
75 g	wholemeal plain flour,	3 oz
75 g	plain flour, plus extra for rolling	3 oz
	pinch salt	
5 ml	mixed herbs	1 teaspoon
75 g	margarine,	3 oz
30–45 ml	water	2–3 tablespoons

For the filling:
1	medium onion	1
30 ml	sunflower oil	2 tablespoons
400 g	can chopped tomatoes	13 oz
30 ml	tomato purée	2 tablespoons
175 g	salami	6 oz
1	small green pepper	1
50 g	Cheddar cheese	2 oz
	salt and freshly ground pepper	

Equipment you will need:
Large mixing bowl, rolling pin, 23 cm (9-inch) deep loose-bottomed flan tin, chopping board, knife, medium saucepan, wooden spoon, can opener, grater, plate.

PIZZA PIE

For a tasty lunch or supper dish, serve this with a salad.
This is what you do:

1. Heat the oven to Gas Mark 6/200°C/400°F.
2. To make the base, put the flour into the bowl with the salt and herbs, cut the margarine into smaller pieces, then add to the flour. With your fingers rub together until the mixture looks like fine breadcrumbs. Mix in the water to make a smooth but not sticky dough.
3. Turn the dough onto a floured work surface then knead until smooth. With a floured rolling pin, roll out into a circle then fit into the flan tin. Roll over the top to trim the edge. Leave in the refrigerator while making the filling.
4. To make the filling, peel and slice the onion very thinly. Put the oil into the saucepan then put on the stove over a medium heat. Add the onion and cook for 5 minutes until soft.
5. Open the can of tomatoes and add to the pan with the purée, salt and pepper. Bring to the boil then reduce the heat. Simmer for about 15 minutes until very thick, stirring occasionally to stop it catching on the bottom of the pan. Turn off the heat.
6. Remove the skin from the salami and cut into thick slices. Cut the top off the pepper, remove the core and seeds and cut into rings. Coarsely grate the cheese onto a plate.
7. Pour the sauce onto the pizza base. Arrange the salami and pepper on top then scatter over the cheese.
8. Put the pizza in the oven to cook for 35–40 minutes or until the top is golden and the pastry cooked. Remove from the oven, turn off the heat and remove sides of the tin from the pie before serving.

Pizza Pie

Suppers, Snacks and Savouries

SUMMER SALAD

Most of the year you can buy different types of lettuce. Try mixing two varieties, such as iceberg and cos, or a red-leaved lettuce and curly endive.
This is what you do:

1 To make the salad, wash the lettuce leaves and drain them in the colander or press them gently with a clean tea-towel. Tear the leaves into pieces and place in the serving bowl.
2 Either slice the cucumber or cut it into chunks. Scrub the celery and cut into thin slices. Remove any seeds from the pepper and cut into thin slices. Trim and chop the spring onions. Add all these ingredients to the bowl.
3 To make the dressing, put all the ingredients into the jar, screw on the top, and shake until mixed together. Pour the dressing over the salad, then, using two spoons, toss everything together.
4 Sprinkle over the sunflower seeds and serve.

Ingredients – serves 4–6

For the salad:

1 or 2 × ½	lettuce	1
7.5 cm	piece cucumber	3-inch
2	sticks celery	2
½	green pepper	½
½ bunch	spring onions	½ bunch
	handful of sunflower seeds	

For the dressing:

45 ml	sunflower oil	3 tablespoons
15 ml	white wine vinegar	1 tablespoon
	pinch of caster sugar	
	salt and freshly ground pepper	

Equipment you will need:
Colander or tea-towel, serving bowl, chopping board, knife, small screw-top jar, two spoons.

MEXICAN RICE

Serve this dish with crusty bread and a salad. It also makes a good accompaniment to barbecued food.
This is what you do:

1 Slice the top off the pepper, remove the core and seeds, then chop into small pieces. Set aside.
2 Peel and chop the onion, put into the saucepan with the oil. Place the saucepan on the stove and cook gently for 5 minutes or until the onion softens.
3 Add the rice and chopped pepper to the pan and cook for a further 2 minutes. Open the can of tomatoes. Add, with the chilli sauce and the water, to the rice, bring to boiling point then reduce the heat to simmer.
4 Cover the pan and cook for 30 minutes. Stir in the sweetcorn and cook another 5 minutes. Season with salt and pepper. Remove from the stove, turn off the heat and serve.

Ingredients – serves 4–6

1	red pepper	1
1	medium onion	1
30 ml	sunflower oil	2 tablespoons
175 g	brown rice	6 oz
400 g	can chopped tomatoes	13 oz
5 ml	chilli sauce (if liked)	1 teaspoon
150 ml	water	¼ pint
125 g	canned or frozen sweetcorn	4 oz
	salt and freshly ground pepper	

Equipment you will need:
Chopping board, knife, large saucepan with lid, wooden spoon, can opener.

Suppers, Snacks and Savouries

Ingredients — serves 4

4	chicken portions	4
25 g	plain flour	1 oz
	salt and freshly ground pepper	
2	oranges	2
½	lemon	½
1	medium onion	1
45 ml	oil	3 tablespoons
150 ml	chicken stock	¼ pint
10 ml	dark-brown soft sugar	2 teaspoons
25 g	desiccated coconut	1 oz

Equipment you will need:
Kitchen paper, polythene bag, grater, lemon squeezer, chopping board, knife, frying pan, wooden spoon, tongs, casserole dish, foil.

TROPICAL CHICKEN

Mixing fruit with chicken can produce an interesting dish with a tropical flavour.
This is what you do:

1 Heat the oven to Gas Mark 5/190°C/375°F
2 Wash the chicken portions and dry with kitchen paper. Put the flour into the polythene bag and season with salt and pepper. Put each chicken piece into the bag, shake it around to coat in the flour then put to one side.
3 Grate the rind from one of the oranges, then squeeze the juice from both of them. Squeeze the juice from the lemon, and mix in with the orange rind and juice.
4 Peel the onion and chop it very finely.
5 Pour 15 ml (1 tablespoon) of the oil into the frying pan and put onto the stove over a medium heat. Add the onion and cook for 4–5 minutes until soft. Tip into the casserole.
6 Add the rest of the oil to the pan, add the chicken pieces and cook them on each side until golden.
7 Remove the pan from the stove, turn off the heat then transfer the chicken to the casserole dish. Stir the remaining seasoned flour from the bag into the juices in the frying pan. Gradually blend in the orange juice and rind, the lemon juice, stock and the sugar.
8 Put the pan back on the stove and bring the sauce to the boil, stirring all the time. Turn off the heat then pour the stock over the chicken. Season again if necessary with salt and pepper.
9 Cook the caserole in the oven for about 1 hour or until the chicken is tender.
10 While the chicken is cooking, cover the grill rack with foil, sprinkle over the coconut and toast until golden.
11 Remove the chicken from the oven and turn off the heat. Scatter the coconut over the chicken and serve.

TASTY BAKES

Ingredients – makes 12

50 g	blanched almonds	2 oz
125 g	glacé cherries	4 oz
50 g	angelica	2 oz
175 g	butter or margarine, plus extra for greasing	6 oz
175 g	caster sugar	6 oz
3	eggs	3
2.5 ml	almond essence	½ teaspoon
250 g	self-raising flour	8 oz
75 g	mixed peel	3 oz
30 ml	orange juice	2 tablespoons

Equipment you will need:
28 × 18 cm (11 × 7-inch) shallow baking tin,
greaseproof paper, chopping board, knife,
small, medium and large mixing bowls, fork,
wooden spoon, sieve, wire cooling rack.

Ingredients – makes about 30

15 ml	Lyle's golden syrup	1 tablespoon
150 g	butter or margarine, plus extra for greasing	5 oz
125 g	granulated sugar	4 oz
150 g	plain flour	5 oz
75 g	porridge oats	3 oz
50 g	desiccated coconut	2 oz
10 ml	baking powder	2 teaspoons

Equipment you will need:
2 or 3 baking trays,
large saucepan, wooden spoon,
sieve, palette knife,
wire cooling rack.

TUTTI FRUTTI CAKE

This is what you do:

1 Heat the oven to Gas Mark 4/180°C/350°F. Grease the baking tin, line with greaseproof paper and grease again.
2 Chop the almonds, cherries and angelica in small pieces.
3 Put the butter and sugar into the large bowl and beat until light and fluffy. Whisk the eggs with a fork in the small bowl, then, with the essence, gradually beat into the butter and sugar.
4 Sieve the flour in the medium bowl, then fold into the mixture. Add the chopped almonds, cherries, angelica, mixed peel, and finally the orange juice. Spoon into the baking tin.
5 Bake the cake in the oven for 25 minutes; turn down the heat to Gas Mark 3/160°C/325°F and cook for a further 10–15 minutes, when the cake should be risen and golden. Take out of the oven and turn off the heat.
6 Leave to stand for 10 minutes then turn out onto the cooling rack. When cold, cut into 12 pieces.

ANZAC BISCUITS

This is what you do:

1 Heat the oven to Gas Mark 3/160°C/325°F. Lightly grease the baking trays.
2 Put the syrup, butter or margarine and sugar into the saucepan. Place the pan on the stove over a gentle heat. With a wooden spoon, stir ingredients until butter melts.
3 Remove the pan from the stove and turn off the heat. Sieve the flour and add to the pan with the oats, coconut and baking powder, and mix together.
4 Roll the mixture in your hands into about 30 balls and place on baking trays, leaving plenty of room for the biscuits to spread.
5 Bake in the oven for about 20 minutes or until evenly browned. Remove from the oven and turn off the heat.
6 Allow to cool on trays for 2–3 minutes then, using a palette knife, lift them onto the wire cooling rack.

Tutti Frutti Cake

Tasty Bakes

CHOCOLATE CRUNCHIES

Ingredients – makes 12

50 g	butter	2 oz
30 ml	Lyle's golden syrup	2 tablespoons
125 g	milk chocolate drops	4 oz
75 g	cornflakes	3 oz

Equipment you will need:
Medium saucepan, wooden spoon, paper bun cases, tray, teaspoon.

If you like, you can use branflakes instead of cornflakes.
This is what you do:

1 Put the butter, syrup and chocolate drops in the saucepan, place on the stove and heat gently, stirring with the wooden spoon, until melted.
2 Remove from the stove and turn off the heat. Add the cornflakes and mix well.
3 Arrange the paper cases on the tray, then spoon the mixture into them. Leave in the refrigerator until set.

STRAWBERRY MACAROON TARTS

Ingredients – makes 12

For the tarts:

75 g	plain flour, plus extra for rolling	3 oz
75 g	wholemeal plain flour	3 oz
75 g	margarine	3 oz
45–60 ml	water	3–4 tablespoons
	strawberry jam	

For the topping:

2	egg whites	2
125 g	ground almonds	4 oz
75 g	caster sugar	3 oz

Equipment you will need:
2 mixing bowls, tablespoon, rolling pin, 7.5 cm (3-inch) cutter, 12-hole bun tin, teaspoon, whisk, palette knife, wire cooling rack.

This is what you do:

1 Heat the oven to Gas Mark 5/190°C/375°F.
2 To make the tarts, put the flours into the bowl, cut the margarine into smaller pieces, add to bowl, and rub together with your fingertips until the mixture resembles fine breadcrumbs. Add 3–4 tablespoons of water. Turn the dough onto a floured surface, knead until smooth, and roll out with a floured rolling pin.
3 Cut circles of pastry with the cutter and fit them into the bun tin. Spoon a teaspoonful of jam into each pastry case then bake in the oven for 10 minutes.
4 While the jam tarts are cooking, put the egg whites into a clean bowl and whisk until stiff. Using a metal spoon, fold in the ground almonds and sugar. Spoon on top of the jam then return the tarts to the oven for a further 15 minutes until golden.
5 Remove from the oven, turn off the heat and transfer the tarts to the wire rack to cool.

Tasty Bakes

MELTING MOMENTS

	Ingredients – makes 20	
125 g	butter, plus extra for greasing	4 oz
75 g	caster sugar	3 oz
1	egg yolk	1
	a few drops of vanilla essence	
150 g	self-raising flour	5 oz
25 g	cornflakes	1 oz
10	glacé cherries	10

Equipment you will need:
2–3 baking trays, large mixing bowl, wooden spoon, sieve, bowl, chopping board, knife, palette knife, wire cooling rack.

This is what you do:

1. Heat the oven to Gas Mark 5/190°C/375°F. Grease the baking trays.
2. Put the butter and sugar into a bowl and beat together until light and fluffy. Add the egg yolk and essence and beat again.
3. Sieve the flour, gradually add to the bowl, and mix to make a stiff dough. Put in the refrigerator to chill for 15 minutes. Crush the cornflakes with your fingers into a bowl.
4. Divide the dough into 20 pieces and roll each into a ball, flatten slightly and press into the cornflakes.
5. Place well apart on the baking trays. Cut the cherries in half and stick one half on each biscuit. Bake in the oven for 15–20 minutes until golden brown.
6. Remove from the oven, turn off the heat, then transfer the biscuits to a wire rack to cool.

TOLLHOUSE COOKIES

	Ingredients – makes 12	
250 g	plain flour	8 oz
10 ml	baking powder	2 teaspoons
125 g	margarine or butter, plus extra for greasing	4 oz
125 g	granulated sugar	4 oz
1	orange	1
75 g	plain chocolate (drops are suitable)	3 oz
1	egg	1

Equipment you will need:
2 baking trays, sieve, large mixing bowl, spoon, grater, fork, palette knife, wire cooling rack.

These American biscuits were traditionally offered to travellers as they paid their money at the toll-gate.
This is what you do:

1. Heat the oven to Gas Mark 6/200°C/400°F. Grease the baking trays.
2. Sieve the flour and baking powder into a bowl. Cut the margarine or butter into smaller pieces, add to the flour, and rub together with your fingertips until the mixture looks like fine breadcrumbs. Stir in the sugar.
3. Finely grate the orange rind and add to the mixture with the chocolate. Beat the egg and add to the bowl, mixing to a firm dough with a fork.
4. Place the mixture on the baking trays in 12 well-spaced heaps. Bake in the oven for about 15–20 minutes until risen and browned.
5. Remove from the oven and turn off the heat. Transfer the biscuits to the wire rack to cool.

Tasty Bakes

OAT AND CHERRY SQUARES

Ingredients – makes 12

125 g	glacé cherries	4 oz
250 g	porridge oats	8 oz
50 g	wholemeal plain flour	2 oz
125 g	margarine, plus extra for greasing	4 oz
30 ml	Lyle's golden syrup	2 tablespoons
125 g	light-brown soft sugar	4 oz

Equipment you will need:
28 × 18 cm (11 × 7-inch) shallow baking tin, chopping board, knife, large mixing bowl, small saucepan, wooden spoon, fish slice, wire cooling rack.

A quick and easy recipe to prepare.

This is what you do:

1 Heat the oven to Gas Mark 5/190°C/375°F. Grease the baking tin.

2 Cut the cherries into small pieces and put into a bowl with the porridge oats and flour.

3 Put the margarine, syrup and sugar in the saucepan, place on the stove and heat gently until the sugar has dissolved.

4 Remove the pan from the stove, turn off the heat then pour the mixture into the bowl and mix all the ingredients together. Spoon into the tin and level. Bake in the oven for 20 minutes or until golden. Remove from the oven and turn off the heat.

5 While the mixture is still warm, cut into squares. Lift onto a wire rack and leave to cool.

FRUIT AND NUT COOKIES

Ingredients – makes 20

75 g	plain flour	3 oz
75 g	porridge oats	3 oz
50 g	butter or margarine, plus extra for greasing	2 oz
125 g	light-brown soft sugar	4 oz
25 g	chopped mixed nuts	1 oz
50 g	raisins	2 oz
2.5 ml	ground cinnamon	½ teaspoon
30 ml	milk	2 tablespoons

Equipment you will need:
2 baking trays, large mixing bowl, wooden spoon, palette knife, wire cooling rack.

These crunchy biscuits are very easy to make and taste delicious.

This is what you do:

1 Heat the oven to Gas Mark 6/200°C/400°F. Grease the baking trays.

2 Put the flour and oats into a bowl, cut the butter into smaller pieces and, using your fingertips, rub them together until the mixture looks like breadcrumbs.

3 Add the sugar, nuts, raisins and cinnamon then mix to a firm dough with the milk.

4 Divide the mixture into 20 heaps. Roll each into a ball, place well apart on the baking tray and flatten with your fingers.

5 Bake in the oven for about 8–10 minutes or until golden. Take out of the oven, turn off the heat then lift the biscuits onto the wire rack to cool.

Oat and Cherry Squares

Tasty Bakes

PEANUT BUTTER BISCUITS

Most children like peanut butter, so here it is in a biscuit recipe.

Ingredients – makes 24

125 g	soft margarine, plus extra for greasing	4 oz
125 g	smooth peanut butter	4 oz
175 g	light-brown soft sugar	6 oz
1	egg	1
175 g	wholemeal plain flour	6 oz
1.25 ml	bicarbonate of soda	1/4 teaspoon
2.5 ml	baking powder	1/2 teaspoon
50 g	unsalted peanuts	2 oz

Equipment you will need:
2 baking trays, 2 large mixing bowls, wooden spoon, sieve, palette knife, wire cooling rack.

This is what you do:

1 Heat the oven to Gas Mark 5/190°C/375°F. Grease the baking trays.
2 Put the margarine, peanut butter and sugar into a bowl and beat until smooth. Add the egg and beat again.
3 In another bowl, sieve together the flour, bicarbonate of soda and baking powder then fold into the butter mixture. Chill the dough for 30 minutes.
4 Divide the dough into 24, and roll into balls with your hands. Place on the baking trays and flatten slightly. Press the nuts on top, then bake for 12–15 minutes in the oven.
5 Remove from the oven, turn off the heat, then transfer the biscuits to the cooling rack.

APRICOT AND RAISIN BUNS

These little buns are ideal for packing into lunch boxes.

Ingredients – makes 12

250 g	self-raising flour	8 oz
5 ml	ground cinnamon	1 teaspoon
125 g	margarine, plus extra for greasing	4 oz
50 g	light-brown soft sugar	2 oz
50 g	semi-dried apricots	2 oz
50 g	raisins	2 oz
1	egg	1

Equipment you will need:
12-hole bun tin, sieve, medium mixing bowl, knife, chopping board, wooden spoon, small mixing bowl, palette knife, wire cooling rack.

This is what you do:

1 Heat the oven to Gas Mark 6/200°C/400°F. Grease the bun tin.
2 Sieve the flour and cinnamon into the medium bowl. Cut the margarine into small pieces, add to flour and rub it in with your fingertips until it looks like bread-crumbs. Stir in the sugar.
3 Chop the apricots then add, with the raisins, to the bowl. Beat the egg in the small mixing bowl then stir into the mixture to make a soft dough. Spoon the mixture into the bun tin and bake for 15–20 minutes until risen and golden.
4 Remove from the oven, turn off the heat and transfer to the wire rack to cool.

Tasty Bakes

Ingredients — makes about 20

For the base:

2	eggs	2
125 g	soft margarine, plus extra for greasing	4 oz
125 g	caster sugar	4 oz
150 g	self-raising flour	5 oz
25 g	desiccated coconut	1 oz

For the topping:

1	egg white	1
50 g	demerara sugar	2 oz
50 g	desiccated coconut	2 oz

Equipment you will need:
28 × 18 cm (11 × 7-inch) shallow baking tin, greaseproof paper, 2 large mixing bowls, wooden spoon, whisk, metal spoon, wire cooling rack, knife.

Ingredients — makes 12

50 g	walnut pieces	2 oz
150 g	wholemeal self-raising flour	5 oz
175 g	light-brown soft sugar	6 oz
125 g	margarine, plus extra for greasing	4 oz
75 g	plain chocolate	3 oz
2	eggs	2
2.5 ml	vanilla essence	½ teaspoon

Equipment you will need:
28 × 18 cm (11 × 7-inch) shallow cake tin, chopping board, knife, large mixing bowl, medium saucepan, medium mixing bowl, small mixing bowl, wooden spoon, wire cooling rack, palette knife.

COCONUT BARS

This is what you do:

1 Heat the oven to Gas Mark 4/180°C/350°F. Grease the baking tin, line with greaseproof paper then grease again.

2 To make the base, put the eggs, margarine, sugar, flour and coconut into a bowl and beat together until smooth and creamy. Turn into the baking tin and level out.

3 To make the topping, put the egg white into a clean bowl and whisk until stiff. With a metal spoon, fold in the demerara sugar and coconut then carefully spread over the top of the cake. Bake in the oven for 25–30 minutes or until the top is firm and golden brown.

4 Take out of the oven, turn off the heat and cool a little. Turn onto the wire rack and peel off the lining paper then turn the cake topping-side up. When completely cool, cut into bars.

BROWNIES

This is what you do:

1 Heat the oven to Gas Mark 4/180°C/350°F. Grease the cake tin.

2 Chop the walnuts into small pieces. Put the flour and sugar into the large mixing bowl.

3 Half-fill the saucepan with water, put on the stove and bring to the boil. Lower the heat, until it is simmering. Put the margarine and chocolate into the medium bowl and stand over the pan of simmering water until both have melted. Turn off the heat.

4 Pour the chocolate mixture into the bowl with the flour and sugar. Beat the eggs in the small bowl and add to the large bowl with the essence and walnuts. Beat until smooth then pour into the tin.

5 Bake in the oven for 30–35 minutes until the cake is risen and beginning to leave the sides of the tin. Remove from the oven and turn off the heat. Leave to cool then cut into 12 squares before removing with a palette knife.

Tasty Bakes

CHOCOLATE MUESLI FINGERS

Ingredients – makes 10		
125 g	butter	4 oz
30 ml	Lyle's golden syrup	2 tablespoons
300 g	muesli	10 oz
125 g	demerara sugar	4 oz
50 g	wholemeal self-raising flour	2 oz
125 g	milk chocolate drops	4 oz

Equipment you will need:
28 × 18 cm (11 × 7-inch) shallow baking tin, medium saucepan, wooden spoon, wire cooling rack, small saucepan, medium bowl, knife.

This is what you do:

1 Heat the oven to Gas Mark 4/180°C/350°F. Grease the baking tin.
2 Put the butter and golden syrup into the medium saucepan. Put on the stove and heat gently until melted. Remove from the stove and turn off the heat.
3 Stir in the muesli, sugar and flour, then turn into the tin, level out and press down. Bake for 25 minutes in the oven.
4 Take out of the oven and turn off the heat. Cut down the centre lengthways then across into fingers.
5 When cool, you may need to cut the muesli fingers again before putting them on the cooling rack.
6 Half-fill the small saucepan with water, place on the stove and bring to the boil. Lower the heat, until it is simmering. Put the chocolate drops in the bowl and stand over the pan of simmering water until melted. Spread over the fingers then leave to set.

ECCLES CAKES

Ingredients – makes 8–10		
25 g	butter, plus extra for greasing	1 oz
25 g	light-brown sugar	1 oz
25 g	mixed peel	1 oz
50 g	currants	2 oz
1.25 ml	mixed spice	1/4 teaspoon
200 g	puff pastry, thawed	7 oz
	flour, for rolling	
	caster sugar, for sprinkling	

Equipment you will need:
Baking tray, mixing bowl, wooden spoon, rolling pin, 10 cm (4-inch) biscuit cutter, fork, pastry brush, palette knife, wire cooling rack.

This is what you do:

1 Heat the oven to Gas Mark 7/220°C/425°F. Grease the baking tray.
2 Put the butter and sugar into the bowl and beat together until creamy. Stir in the mixed peel, currants and spice.
3 With a floured rolling pin, roll out the pastry on a floured surface and stamp out 8–10 rounds with the cutter.
4 Divide the fruit filling between the rounds, and dampen the edges of the pastry with water. Draw them up into the centre, and pinch them together to seal. Turn each cake over and flatten with the rolling pin. Prick the top with a fork. Lightly brush the tops with water then sprinkle with caster sugar. Place on the baking tray and cook in the oven for about 15 minutes.
5 Remove from the oven, turn off the heat, and transfer the cakes to the wire rack to cool.

Chocolate Muesli Fingers, Eccles Cakes and Lemon Shorties

Tasty Bakes

LEMON SHORTIES

	Ingredients – makes 18	
125 g	butter	4 oz
150 g	plain flour	5 oz
25 g	ground rice	1 oz
1	lemon	1
50 g	caster sugar	2 oz

Equipment you will need:
Medium mixing bowl, grater,
20 cm (8-inch) flan tin,
fork, knife.

Easy to make, this shortbread has a tang of lemon.
This is what you do:

1. Heat the oven to Gas Mark 4/180°C/350°F.
2. Cut the butter into small pieces, put it into a bowl with the flour and ground rice, and rub together with your fingers until well blended.
3. Finely grate the lemon rind then add, with the sugar, to the mixture. Knead the ingredients together until they are almost like a dough.
4. Turn the mixture into the flan tin and press down evenly. Mark round the edge with a fork then bake in the oven for 25 minutes until light golden.
5. Take out of the oven and turn off the heat. Cool slightly then cut through the biscuit into 8 triangles. When cool, remove from the tin.

CHERRY ALMOND ROCK CAKES

	Ingredients – makes 12	
125 g	glacé cherries	4 oz
75 g	margarine, plus extra for greasing	3 oz
175 g	wholemeal self-raising flour	6 oz
75 g	caster sugar	3 oz
50 g	ground almonds	2 oz
1	egg	1
30 ml	milk	2 tablespoons

Equipment you will need:
Baking tray, chopping
board, knife, large and small
mixing bowl, spoon, palette
knife, wire cooling rack.

This is what you do:

1. Heat the oven to Gas Mark 5/190°C/375°F. Grease the baking tray.
2. Chop the cherries into small pieces.
3. Cut the margarine into small pieces and put into a mixing bowl with the flour. Rub together with the fingertips until the mixture looks like breadcrumbs. Stir in the sugar, ground almonds and cherries.
4. In a small bowl beat the egg and milk together then add to the other ingredients and work together to form a stiff mixture.
5. Place the mixture in small heaps on the baking tray then bake in the oven for 15 minutes or until they are firm and golden.
6. Remove from the oven, turn the oven off then transfer the cakes to the wire rack to cool.

Tasty Bakes

Ingredients – makes 8

75 g	margarine	3 oz
15 ml	Lyle's golden syrup	1 tablespoon
50 g	demerara sugar	2 oz
125 g	porridge oats	4 oz
125 g	wholemeal plain flour	4 oz
45 ml	marmalade	3 tablespoons

Equipment you will need:
18 cm (7-inch) flan tin, medium
saucepan, wooden spoon, knife.

Ingredients – makes 8–9

250 g	wholemeal self-raising flour, plus extra for rolling	8 oz
	pinch salt	
5 ml	baking powder	1 teaspoon
50 g	margarine, plus extra for greasing	2 oz
25 g	caster sugar	1 oz
50 g	currants	2 oz
150 ml	milk, plus extra for glazing	¼ pint

Equipment you will need:
Baking tray, large mixing bowl,
spoon, knife, rolling pin,
6 cm (2½-inch) cutter,
pastry brush, palette knife,
wire cooling rack.

MARMALADE FLAPJACKS

This is what you do:

1. Heat the oven to Gas Mark 4/180°C/350°F. Grease the flan tin.
2. Put the margarine, golden syrup and sugar in the saucepan and place on the stove. Heat gently until the margarine melts.
3. Remove from the stove, turn off the heat and mix in the oats and flour.
4. Spread half of the oat mixture over the base of the flan tin. Spread the marmalade on top then cover with the rest of the oat mixture. Press down well.
5. Bake in the oven for 20 minutes. Remove from the oven, turn off the heat and leave to stand a few minutes.
6. While still warm, run a knife around the edge then cut into 8 portions. When cold, lift out of the tin.

FRUIT SCONES

This is what you do:

1. Heat the oven to Gas Mark 8/230°C/450°F. Grease the baking tray.
2. Put the flour, salt and baking powder into the mixing bowl, cut the margarine into smaller pieces and, with your fingers, rub together until the mixture looks like breadcrumbs.
3. Stir in the sugar and currants then, using a knife, mix in the milk to give a soft dough. Turn the dough onto a floured surface and knead lightly to remove any cracks.
4. Roll the dough out to 2 cm (¾-inch) thickness. Using the cutter dipped in flour, cut out the scones. Gather up the scraps, knead together, re-roll and cut out more scones.
5. Place the scones on the baking tray then brush the tops with a little milk. Bake near the top of the oven for 8–10 minutes until well risen and golden brown.
6. Remove from the oven and turn off the heat. Transfer to a wire rack to cool. To serve, cut in half and spread with butter.

Tasty Bakes

CHOCOLATE CHIP COOKIES

Ingredients – makes 20

125 g	butter, plus extra for greasing	4 oz
250 g	light-brown soft sugar	8 oz
1	egg	1
5 ml	vanilla essence	1 teaspoon
75 g	wholemeal plain flour	3 oz
25 g	cocoa	1 oz
125 g	chocolate drops, plain or milk	4 oz

Equipment you will need:
2–3 baking trays, large mixing bowl, wooden spoon, dessertspoon, palette knife, wire cooling rack.

This is what you do:

1 Heat the oven to Gas Mark 5/190°C/375°F. Grease the baking trays.
2 Put the butter and sugar into the bowl and beat together until light and fluffy. Beat in the egg and essence. Sieve the flour and cocoa and add to the bowl with the chocolate drops. Add in the bran from the flour (in the sieve) as well. Mix well.
3 Take dessertspoons of the mixture, roll into balls then place well apart on the baking trays. Bake for 10–12 minutes.
4 Take out of the oven, turn off the heat, then leave the biscuits to stand for 2–3 minutes, before transferring them to the wire rack to cool.

JAM BUTTONS

Ingredients – makes about 16

125 g	margarine or butter, plus extra for greasing	4 oz
125 g	caster sugar	4 oz
	few drops vanilla essence	
1	egg	1
175 g	self-raising flour, plus extra for rolling	6 oz
	raspberry jam	

Equipment you will need:
2 baking trays, large mixing bowl, wooden spoon, greaseproof paper, knife, teaspoon, palette knife, wire cooling rack.

The dough for these biscuits is refrigerated, so you can make up the mixture well before you want to cook the biscuits. For a change, try lemon curd instead of jam.
This is what you do:

1 Heat the oven to Gas Mark 5/190°C/375°F. Grease the baking trays.
2 Put the margarine or butter and sugar into the bowl and beat together until light and creamy. Add the essence, egg and a spoonful of flour to stop the mixture curdling.
3 Sieve the rest of the flour, add to the bowl and mix to make a dough. On a floured surface, roll the dough into a thick sausage shape. Wrap in greaseproof paper and chill for at least 2 hours.
4 Cut the dough into 5 mm (¼-inch) slices and place them well apart on the baking trays. Make an indentation in each slice with the end of the wooden spoon then place a small blob of jam in the hollow. Bake in the oven for 15 minutes until golden.
5 Remove from the oven, turn off the heat and transfer the biscuits to the wire rack to cool.

Tasty Bakes

BUTTERFLY CAKES

A very special addition to birthday tea parties.

Ingredients – makes 12

For the cakes:
75 g	butter or margarine	3 oz
75 g	caster sugar	3 oz
½	lemon	½
1	egg	1
150 g	self-raising flour	5 oz

For the filling:
75 g	butter	3 oz
175 g	icing sugar, plus extra for coating	6 oz
30 ml	milk	2 tablespoons

Equipment you will need:
12 paper bun cases, 12–hole bun tin, mixing bowl, wooden spoon, grater, lemon squeezer, sieve, spoon, wire cooling rack, knife, teaspoon.

This is what you do:
1. Heat the oven to Gas Mark 5/190°C/375°F. Put the paper cases in the bun tin.
2. Put the butter or margarine and sugar into a bowl and beat together until light and fluffy.
3. Finely grate the lemon rind, squeeze the juice and beat into the mixture with the egg.
4. Sieve the flour then fold into the mixture. Spoon into the paper cases then bake in the oven for 12–15 minutes until golden and springy to touch.
5. Remove the cakes from the oven, turn off the heat then place on the wire rack to cool.
6. Make up the buttercream filling by putting the butter into a bowl. Sieve the icing sugar onto the butter, add the milk, and beat together until smooth and creamy.
7. When the buns are cool, cut a slice from the top of each and halve each slice. Spoon a teaspoonful of buttercream onto each cake then stick the small cake slices into the buttercream at an angle to make the 'wings'. Sieve a little icing sugar over the finished cakes.

DROP SCONES

These scones are best eaten warm and are delicious with butter and golden syrup.

This is what you do:

Ingredients – makes about 16

75 g	plain flour	3 oz
	pinch salt	
5 ml	baking powder	1 teaspoon
75 g	plain wholemeal flour	3 oz
25 g	caster sugar	1 oz
1	egg	1
175 ml	milk	6 fl oz
	oil for frying	

Equipment you will need:
Sieve, medium mixing bowl, spoon, fork, small mixing bowl, whisk, heavy-based frying pan, tablespoon, palette knife, tea-towel, wire cooling rack.

1. Sieve the plain flour, salt and baking powder into the medium bowl. Stir in the wholemeal flour and the sugar.
2. Beat the egg with a fork in the small bowl and pour, with a little of the milk, onto the flour mixture. Gradually add the rest of the milk, and whisk together until you have a smooth and thick batter.
3. Place the frying pan over a medium heat, spooning ½ teaspoon of oil onto it for each batch. Tilt to cover pan. To test if the pan is hot enough, drop a little batter onto it, and it should begin to bubble within 1 minute.
4. Drop 3 separate tablespoonfuls of batter onto the hot pan, to make 3 scones. Cook for 1–2 minutes then, using the palette knife, carefully turn each scone over. The cooked side should be golden. Cook the second side for 1 minute or until golden.
5. Remove the cooked scones from the pan and place them on a clean tea-towel over a cooling rack. Wrap the towel around the scones to keep in the steam and prevent them from becoming dry.
6. Continue making scones in the same way, until the batter is used up, greasing the pan a little before cooking each batch. Turn off the heat and serve the scones warm.

DELICIOUS DESSERTS

FRUIT KEBABS

Ingredients – serves 4

½	lemon	½
1	large apple	1
2	bananas	2
1	large orange	1
½	small pineapple	½
50 g	unsalted butter	2 oz
40 g	demerara sugar	1½ oz

Equipment you will need:
Lemon squeezer, large bowl, chopping board, knife, 8 small wooden skewers, small saucepan, wooden spoon, foil, pastry brush.

You can use a variety of seasonal fruit for these kebabs, or mix some fresh fruit with canned fruit.

This is what you do:

1 Squeeze the juice from the lemon and pour into a bowl.
2 Wash the apple, cut into quarters, remove the core then cut into chunks. Toss these in the lemon juice. Peel the bananas, cut them into 2.5 cm (1-inch) slices and toss them in the lemon juice.
3 Cut all the skin and pith away from the orange then cut the orange into quarters, then each quarter into half.
4 Cut off the skin from the pineapple, cut out the woody centre then cut the pineapple into 2.5 cm (1-inch) chunks.
5 Thread pieces of fruit alternately onto the skewers.
6 Put the butter and sugar into a small saucepan and place on the stove over a low heat, stir until melted. Turn off the heat.
7 Heat the grill to moderate, cover the grill pan with a piece of foil, then arrange the kebabs and brush over the butter and sugar mixture.
8 Cook the kebabs under the grill for 6–8 minutes, turning them so that they cook evenly and do not burn.
9 Turn off the grill and serve the kebabs with the buttery juices that collect on the foil.

Fruit Kebabs

Delicious Desserts

BANANA CRUNCH FLAN

With its biscuit base and lemony yogurt filling, this dessert will impress all the family when you serve it up.

This is what you do:

Ingredients – serves 6–8

For the base:
250 g	digestive biscuits	8 oz
75 g	butter	3 oz
25 g	plain chocolate	1 oz

For the filling:
1	lemon jelly	1
150 ml	water	¼ pint
25 g	caster sugar	1 oz
2	bananas	2
300 ml	carton natural yogurt	10.6 fl oz

For the decoration:
1	banana	1
15 ml	lemon juice	1 tablespoon
1	chocolate flake bar	1

Equipment you will need:
Polythene bag, rolling pin, 2 medium saucepans, wooden spoon, 23 cm (9-inch) flan dish, chopping board, knife, whisk, bowl.

1. To make the base, put the biscuits into the polythene bag and roll them with a rolling pin to crush.
2. Put the butter into a saucepan, place on the stove and melt over a low heat. Remove from the stove, turn off the heat, add the chocolate and let it melt in the hot butter. Stir in the crushed biscuits, then tip into the flan dish.
3. With your fingers press the biscuit mixture evenly around the sides and over the base of the dish, then put into the refrigerator to set.
4. To make the filling, put the jelly into a saucepan with the water and put on the stove over a low heat and leave to dissolve. Remove from the stove, turn off the heat, stir in the sugar and allow to cool.
5. Peel and slice the bananas, then place them on the biscuit base of the flan. Whisk the yogurt into the cooled jelly then pour the mixture over the bananas. Return the flan to the refrigerator to set.
6. To decorate the flan, slice the last banana, toss in a bowl with the lemon juice, then arrange around the edge of the flan. Crumble the flake bar over the top.

Delicious Desserts

Ingredients — serves 6

For the base:

75 g	plain flour, plus extra for rolling	3 oz
75 g	wholemeal plain flour	3 oz
75 g	margarine	3 oz
45 ml	water	3 tablespoons

For the filling:

250 g	Lyle's golden syrup	8 oz
75 g	natural breadcrumbs	3 oz
25 g	desiccated coconut	1 oz
1/2	lemon	1/2

Equipment you will need:
Large mixing bowl, knife,
rolling pin, 20 cm (8-inch)
loose-bottomed flan tin,
medium saucepan, grater,
lemon squeezer, wooden spoon.

TREACLE TART

Coconut has been added to the filling to give it an interesting flavour. Serve with natural yogurt or custard.
This is what you do:

1 Put the flours into the bowl. Cut the margarine into small pieces, add to flour and, with your fingertips, rub them together until they look like breadcrumbs. Add the water, and mix together with a knife. Gather the dough up with your fingers and knead lightly on a floured surface until smooth.

2 Roll out the pastry and fit into the flan tin. Without stretching the sides, press the pastry into the tin. Roll over the top of the tin to neaten the edges. Cut off the surplus pastry.

3 Heat the oven to Gas Mark 6/200°C/400°F.

4 To make the filling, put the golden syrup, breadcrumbs and coconut into the saucepan. Grate the rind from the lemon and squeeze the juice then add to the pan. Place on the stove and heat gently, stirring with a wooden spoon until all the ingredients are mixed together. Turn off the heat and pour the filling into the pastry case.

5 Bake in the oven for about 25 minutes or until the filling is set and golden. Remove from the oven, turn off the heat, and serve the tart warm.

Delicious Desserts

Ingredients — serves 4

For the pancakes:

50 g	wholemeal plain flour	2 oz
50 g	plain flour	2 oz
I	egg	I
300 ml	milk	½ pint
15 g	butter	½ oz
	oil for frying	

For the sauce:

50 g	unsalted butter	2 oz
125 g	light-brown soft sugar	4 oz
125 g	Lyle's golden syrup	4 oz
5 ml	cornflour	I teaspoon
30 ml	milk	2 tablespoons

Equipment you will need:
Sieve, medium bowl, wooden
spoon, small saucepan, whisk,
18 cm (7-inch) frying pan,
tablespoon, palette knife,
ovenproof plate, medium
saucepan, small bowl.

PANCAKES WITH BUTTERSCOTCH SAUCE

You can make two batches of these pancakes and store some in the freezer. Try the sauce over ice cream too.

This is what you do:

1 Heat the oven to Gas Mark 2/150°C/300°F.

2 Sieve the flours into the bowl, adding any bran left in the sieve. Make a well in the centre and add the egg. Beat well with the wooden spoon. Gradually whisk in the milk to make a smooth batter. Turn off the heat.

3 Put the butter in a saucepan and place on the stove. Heat gently to melt then whisk it into the batter. Turn off the heat.

4 To make the pancakes, put the frying pan on the stove over a moderately high heat, add ½ teaspoon oil and tilt to cover the surface of the pan. Take the pan off the heat, pour in 3 tablespoonfuls of the batter, swirl it around then return to the heat. When the top looks set, loosen the sides with a palette knife and turn the pancake over to cook on the other side for about 30 seconds. Turn the pancake onto the ovenproof plate.

5 Continue making pancakes in the same way until all the batter is used up. Turn off the heat. Put into a warm oven, Gas Mark 3/160°C/325°F, covered with foil to keep warm while you make the sauce.

6 Put the unsalted butter into the medium saucepan. Place on the stove over a low heat to melt, then add the sugar and syrup and stir until the sugar dissolves. Bring to the boil, then leave to simmer for 3 minutes without stirring. In a small bowl blend the cornflour with the milk, stir into the sauce and heat for I minute. Remove from the stove and turn off the heat.

7 To serve, take the pancakes out of the oven and turn the oven off. Fold the pancakes into quarters, pour the sauce over and serve at once.

Pancakes with Butterscotch Sauce

Delicious Desserts

Ingredients – serves 4–6

60 ml	Lyle's golden syrup	4 tablespoons
1	lemon	1
125 g	butter or margarine, plus extra for greasing	4 oz
125 g	light-brown soft sugar	4 oz
2	eggs	2
75 g	self-raising flour	3 oz
75 g	wholemeal self-raising flour	3 oz
	a little milk	

Equipment you will need:
Large saucepan with lid, saucer, 900 ml (1½-pint) bowl, tablespoon, grater, large and small mixing bowls, wooden spoon, fork, sieve, foil, string, large plate.

STEAMED SYRUP SPONGE

Served with custard, this is the perfect pudding for cold winter days.

This is what you do:

1. Half-fill the saucepan with water, place an old saucer upside-down on the bottom then put the saucepan on the stove with the lid on, and bring the water to the boil. Grease the 900 ml (1½-pint) bowl and spoon the golden syrup into the bottom of it.
2. Finely grate the rind from the lemon and set aside.
3. Put the butter or margarine and sugar into the large mixing bowl then beat together until pale and fluffy. Beat the eggs in the small mixing bowl, and gradually add to the butter and sugar mixture, beating well after each addition.
4. Sieve the white flour then add to the mixture with the wholemeal flour and the lemon rind, mixing well. If the mixture is too stiff, add a little milk to give a softer consistency.
5. Spoon the mixture into the 900 ml (1½-pint) bowl over the syrup. Butter a piece of greaseproof paper or foil then use to cover the bowl, tying a piece of string around the rim to secure it.
6. Remove saucepan from the heat, place the bowl on top of the saucer in the saucepan, cover with the lid, return to the heat and simmer for 2 hours. Check during cooking to make sure that there is plenty of water in the saucepan.
7. To serve, remove the pan from the stove, turn off the heat and, using oven gloves, lift the pudding out of the water. Remove the string and paper or foil. Place a plate over the pudding then, holding both the plate and bowl, turn the bowl upside-down and the pudding will drop onto the plate. Serve hot.

Delicious Desserts

RICE PUDDING CRACKLE

Branflakes or cornflakes are an ideal topping for this dessert that is so quick to make.

This is what you do:

Ingredients — serves 4

For the pudding:

439 g	can rice pudding	15½ oz
150 ml	whipping cream	¼ pint

For the topping:

15 g	butter	½ oz
15 ml	Lyle's golden syrup	1 tablespoon
25 g	branflakes	1 oz

Equipment you will need:
Can opener, 2 medium bowls,
whisk, 4 sundae dishes,
medium saucepan, spoon.

1 Open the can of rice pudding and put into a bowl. Pour the cream into the other bowl and whisk until thick, fold into the rice pudding then spoon into 4 sundae dishes.
2 Put the butter and golden syrup into the saucepan, place on the stove and melt over a low heat. Remove from the stove and turn off the heat.
3 Stir the branflakes into the mixture then spoon it over the rice pudding. Refrigerate for about 30 minutes or until the topping is set.

ORANGE CHOCOLATE MOUSSE

This is what you do:

Ingredients — serves 6

175 g	plain chocolate	6 oz
1	orange	1
50 g	unsalted butter	2 oz
2	eggs	2
25 g	caster sugar	1 oz
75 ml	double cream	5 tablespoons

Equipment you will need:
Grater, medium saucepan,
1 large and 2 small mixing bowls,
lemon squeezer, wooden spoon,
whisk, 6 ramekins.

1 Grate 25 g (1 oz) of chocolate and set aside for decoration.
2 Half-fill the saucepan with water, put onto the stove and heat until boiling. Lower the heat until the water is simmering. Break up the rest of the chocolate into the large bowl and place in the saucepan until it melts.
3 While waiting for the chocolate to melt, grate the rind from the orange and squeeze the juice.
4 Remove the chocolate from the pan, turn off the heat. Beat in the butter and add the orange rind and juice.
5 Separate the egg whites and yolks into the two small bowls. Whisk the whites until stiff. Add the sugar to the yolks and whisk until pale and creamy.
6 Beat the egg yolk mixture into the chocolate mixture, then fold in the whisked egg whites. Pour the mixture into the 6 dishes and chill until set.
7 To serve, whip the cream until thick, divide between the chocolate mousses then sprinkle over the reserved grated chocolate.

Delicious Desserts

Ingredients – serves 6

25 g	plain chocolate	1 oz
90 ml	cornflour	6 tablespoons
900 ml	milk	1½ pints
50 g	caster sugar	2 oz

few drops vanilla essence
few drops almond essence
few drops pink food colouring

Equipment you will need:
Small and medium saucepan, 2 medium mixing bowls, large measuring jug, wooden spoon, whisk, 900 ml (1½-pint) jelly mould, serving plate.

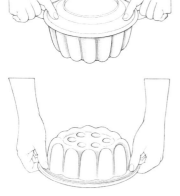

STRIPY BLANCMANGE

You can make blancmange all one colour, but three flavours are more fun.

This is what you do:

1. Half-fill the small saucepan with water, place on the stove and bring to the boil. Lower the heat, and when the water is simmering, put the chocolate in a bowl, then sit it in the pan over the simmering water until it melts. Remove the bowl from the pan and turn off the heat.
2. Put the cornflour into the other mixing bowl, add 60 ml (4 tablespoons) of milk and blend together with the wooden spoon.
3. Pour the rest of the milk into the medium saucepan and put on the stove. Heat until it reaches boiling point, then remove from the heat and pour onto the blended cornflour, stirring all the time. Carefully pour the mixture back into the saucepan, return to the stove and bring back to the boil, stirring all the time as it thickens. Continue to cook for 2 minutes over a low heat.
4. Stir in the sugar. Remove from the stove, and turn off the heat.
5. Pour one-third of the custard onto the chocolate and whisk together. Pour another third back into the other mixing bowl and add the vanilla essence. Then flavour the final portion left in the saucepan with the almond essence and colour it with a few drops of pink food colouring. Now, one after the other, pour the three flavours into the mould to give three layers. As you pour each variety, leave it a moment or two, to cool a little and begin to set.
6. Allow the blancmange to cool, then refrigerate until ready to serve.
7. To serve, dip the mould in a bowl of hot water for about 10 seconds, place a plate over it, then, holding both the plate and the mould, turn the mould upside-down and the blancmange will drop onto the plate.

Stripy Blancmange

Delicious Desserts

PEACH CRISP

	Ingredients – serves 6	
75 g	butter, plus extra for greasing	3 oz
30 ml	Lyle's golden syrup	2 tablespoons
65 g	rice crispies	2½ oz
150 ml	whipping cream, or thick Greek yogurt	¼ pint
400 g	can peach slices, or 2 fresh peaches, sliced	14 oz

Equipment you will need:
20 cm (8-inch) loose-bottomed flan tin, greaseproof paper, large saucepan, wooden spoon, serving plate, bowl, whisk, can opener, sieve.

This is what you do:

1 Grease the flan tin and then place a circle of greaseproof paper over the base.
2 Put the butter and golden syrup into the saucepan and heat gently until melted, stirring with the wooden spoon.
3 Stir in the rice crispies and mix well. Turn off the heat, tip the mixture into the prepared tin and level the crispy mixture by pressing down slightly with the back of the spoon. Place in the refrigerator for about 2 hours until set.
4 Push the base out of the tin, turn upside-down onto a serving plate and peel away the paper.
5 If using cream, put it into a bowl and whisk until it becomes thick. Spread the cream or Greek yogurt over the crispy base.
6 Open the can of peaches and tip them into the sieve over the sink to allow the juice to drain away. (If you would like to save the juice to use in a jelly, drain the peaches over a bowl.)
7 Arrange the peach slices on top of the cream or yogurt and serve the dessert.

TOFFEE TOAST

	Ingredients – serves 4	
4	slices soft batch bread	4
50 g	caster sugar	2 oz
30 ml	Lyle's golden syrup	2 tablespoons
50 g	butter	2 oz

Equipment you will need:
Toaster, bread board, knife, large frying pan, tongs, wire cooling rack.

Once they have tried this, served with yogurt, the rest of the family will be asking for more.

This is what you do:

1 Toast the bread then cut each slice in half diagonally.
2 Put the rest of the ingredients into the pan and heat gently until the sugar has melted, then continue to heat until the mixture turns golden. Turn off the heat.
3 Using tongs, dip each piece of toast in the toffee, turning to coat each side.
4 Lift out and cool for a few minutes on the wire rack before serving.

Delicious Desserts

BAKED APPLES

Serve this popular dessert with thick yogurt.
This is what you do:

Ingredients – serves 4		
4	medium cooking apples	4
25 g	raisins	1 oz
25 g	demerara sugar	1 oz
45 ml	water	3 tablespoons

Equipment you will need:
Apple corer, sharp knife, ovenproof dish, spoon.

1. Heat the oven to Gas Mark 5/190°C/375°F.
2. Wash the apples then remove their centres using the corer. Make a cut into the skin around the middle of each apple; this stops them splitting and exploding in the oven.
3. Stand the apples in the ovenproof dish, fill the centres with the raisins and half of the sugar and sprinkle over the rest of the sugar. Pour the water around the apples and bake in the oven for about 25–30 minutes, or until the apples are soft when tested with the point of a sharp knife. Remove from the oven and turn off the heat.

Variations: A mixture of chopped dates or dried apricots and nuts, or just blackberries, makes a delicious filling, too.

EVE'S PUDDING

Serve this pudding with custard or cream on cold winter days.
This is what you do:

Ingredients – serves 4–6		
For the base:		
500 g	cooking apples	1 lb
50 g	demerara sugar	2 oz
For the topping:		
125 g	soft margarine	4 oz
125 g	caster sugar	4 oz
125 g	wholemeal self-raising flour	4 oz
2	eggs	2
	few drops almond essence	

Equipment you will need:
Potato peeler, knife, chopping board, 1.2-litre (2-pint) ovenproof dish, large mixing bowl, wooden spoon.

1. Turn the oven on to Gas Mark 4/180°C/350°F.
2. Peel and core the apples then chop them into chunks. Then put them into the ovenproof dish with the demerara sugar.
3. Put all the ingredients for the topping into a mixing bowl and beat together until smoothly blended.
4. Spoon the mixture over the apples, then level the top of the pudding. Put into the oven to bake for 50–60 minutes or until the top is firm when gently pressed. Take the pudding out of the oven and turn off the heat.

Delicious Desserts

CHOCOLATE FONDUE

	Ingredients – serves 4	
125 g	milk chocolate drops	4 oz
25 g	unsalted butter	1 oz
30 ml	double cream	2 tablespoons
15 ml	Lyle's golden syrup	1 tablespoon
30 ml	tropical fruit juice	2 tablespoons

Equipment you will need:
Small saucepan, wooden spoon, bowl, forks for dipping.

This is a fun way to end a meal, with everyone dipping chunks of cake or pieces of fruit into the warm chocolate sauce.

This is what you do:

1 Put the chocolate drops, butter, cream, syrup and fruit juice in the pan, place on the stove and heat very gently, stirring with the wooden spoon, until the chocolate melts. Beat the mixture until smooth.

2 Turn off the heat and pour into a serving bowl and serve with pieces of fruit or chunks of plain cake.

FRESH FRUIT SALAD

	Ingredients – serves 6	
75 g	light-brown soft sugar	3 oz
300 ml	water	½ pint
1	cinnamon stick	1
½	lemon	½
1	apple	1
1	banana	1
2	oranges	2
125 g	black grapes	4 oz
125 g	green grapes	4 oz
125 g	strawberries	4 oz

Equipment you will need:
Medium saucepan with lid, potato peeler, lemon squeezer, serving bowl, chopping board, knife, sieve, spoon.

The recipe gives you ideas, but you can make the salad with any of your favourite fruits.

This is what you do:

1 Put the sugar, water and cinnamon stick in the saucepan. Peel 2 strips of lemon rind and add to the pan.

2 Put the saucepan on the stove and heat until boiling, then allow the syrup to simmer for 5 minutes. Turn off the heat, cover the pan with a lid and leave to cool.

3 Squeeze the juice from the lemon and pour into the serving bowl.

4 Wash the apple, cut into quarters, remove the core then cut into chunks. Peel and slice the banana then add, with the apple chunks, to the bowl and toss in the lemon juice, to prevent discolouration.

5 Cut away all the peel and pith from the oranges, and remove pips. Cut into segments and put into the bowl.

6 Wash the grapes, cut each one in half and remove the pips and put into the bowl.

7 Wash the strawberries, remove the green stalk then cut in half and add to the rest of the fruit.

8 Strain the syrup over the fruit, mix together, then cover and refrigerate until ready to serve.

chocolate Fondue

SPECIAL OCCASIONS

Ingredients — serves 4

1.25–1.5 kg	spare ribs	3–3½ lb
45 ml	light-brown soft sugar	3 tablespoons
60 ml	soy sauce	4 tablespoons
15 ml	Worcestershire sauce	1 tablespoon
30 ml	red wine vinegar	2 tablespoons
30 ml	tomato ketchup	2 tablespoons
5 ml	mustard	1 teaspoon
150 ml	orange juice	¼ pint

Equipment you will need:
Large roasting tin, bowl,
spoon.

SPICY SPARE RIBS

Serve these ribs with a salad for a tasty, fun meal. The easiest way to eat the ribs is to hold them in your hands. For that special touch, give your guests a little bowl of water with a slice of lemon so that they can rinse their fingers after eating.

This is what you do:

1 Heat the oven to Gas Mark 5/190°C/375°F.
2 Wash the ribs and put into the roasting tin.
3 Mix all the other ingredients together in the bowl then pour over the ribs. Place them in the oven to cook for 1–1¼ hours. Every 15 minutes carefully take the ribs out of the oven and spoon the juices over them. Towards the end of cooking, the juices will disappear, leaving the ribs with a rich glaze.
4 Remove the tin from the oven, turn off the heat and pile the ribs onto a serving plate.

Spicy Spare Ribs

Special Occasions

Ingredients — serves 4

4 × 125 g	large boneless chicken breasts	4 × 4 oz

For the marinade:

30 ml	soy sauce	2 tablespoons
15 ml	sunflower oil	1 tablespoon
5 ml	ground ginger	1 teaspoon
2.5 ml	turmeric	½ teaspoon
5 ml	ground coriander	1 teaspoon
2.5 ml	dark-brown soft sugar	½ teaspoon
	pinch chilli powder	

For the sauce:

40 g	desiccated coconut	1 ½ oz
250 ml	boiling water	8 fl oz
60 ml	peanut butter	4 tablespoons
10 ml	dark-brown soft sugar	2 teaspoons

Equipment you will need:
Chopping board, knife,
2 medium bowls, spoon, sieve,
small saucepan, 8 small
bamboo or wooden skewers,
pastry brush, wooden spoon.

CHINESE SATÉ WITH PEANUT SAUCE

This Indonesian dish is becoming very popular now, particularly with children, who enjoy the peanut sauce. *This is what you do:*

1 Remove the skin from the chicken and cut into 1-inch pieces.

2 Put the soy sauce, sunflower oil, ginger, turmeric, coriander, sugar and chilli powder into a bowl and mix together. Add the chicken pieces and mix well, making sure all the chicken is coated with the spice mixture. Cover the bowl and leave in a refrigerator for 2 hours.

3 In the meantime, put the coconut in a bowl and pour over the boiling water. Cover and leave to stand for 15 minutes.

4 Strain the coconut into a small saucepan, pressing out the liquid. Discard the coconut left in the sieve. Put the rest of the sauce ingredients into the pan and mix well.

5 Thread the pieces of chicken onto the skewers. Heat the grill to moderate and arrange the skewers on the grill rack. Brush with the marinade and grill for about 15 minutes, turning and brushing with the marinade occasionally.

6 While the chicken is cooking put the saucepan on the stove over a low heat and heat slowly, stirring with the wooden spoon. Simmer for 1–2 minutes then turn off the heat. Spoon the thick sauce into a serving bowl.

7 When the chicken is cooked, turn off the grill and serve with the peanut sauce.

Special Occasions

CHINESE CHICKEN WINGS

	Ingredients – serves 4	
12	chicken wings	12
15 ml	dark soy sauce	1 tablespoon
15 ml	Lyle's golden syrup	1 tablespoon
30 ml	tomato purée	2 tablespoons
15 ml	cider vinegar	1 tablespoon
	sesame seeds	

Equipment you will need:
Kitchen paper,
large ovenproof dish,
small bowl, spoon.

Why not make these chinese chicken wings next time you invite some friends round? Serve with rice and prawn crackers for a super party meal.

This is what you do:

1. Heat the oven to Gas Mark 5/190°C/375°F.
2. Wash the chicken wings, dry on kitchen paper, then place in the ovenproof dish.
3. Put the soy sauce, golden syrup, tomato purée and vinegar into the bowl and mix well. Spoon over the chicken. Sprinkle with sesame seeds then bake in the oven for 45 minutes. Remove from the oven and turn off the heat.

BRAZILIAN BEEF

	Ingredients – serves 4	
500 g	braising steak	1 lb
1	large onion	1
30 ml	sunflower oil	2 tablespoons
10 ml	lemon juice	2 teaspoons
300 ml	beef stock	½ pint
5 ml	paprika	1 teaspoon
2.5 ml	ground ginger	½ teaspoon
227 g	can pineapple slices	8 oz
15 ml	cornflour	1 tablespoon
50 g	shelled brazil nuts	2 oz
	salt and freshly ground pepper	

Equipment you will need:
Chopping board, knife, large
saucepan, wooden spoon,
can opener, sieve, small bowl.

Serve this unusual beef casserole with boiled potatoes and green vegetables.

This is what you do:

1. Cut the meat into 4 cm (1 ½-inch) chunks, and peel and chop the onion. Put the oil into the saucepan, and place on the stove over a medium heat.
2. Add the meat and onion to the pan and cook until the meat is browned all over, stirring it around with the wooden spoon.
3. Stir in the lemon juice, stock, paprika, ginger, salt and pepper. Bring to the boil, then reduce the heat, cover pan with lid, and simmer for 1 ½ hours.
4. In the meantime, open the can of pineapple slices, drain the juice into the small bowl and blend with the cornflour. Chop the brazil nuts into small pieces, and cut the pineapple slices into quarters.
5. When the meat is tender, stir in the blended cornflour and the pineapple pieces and simmer for a further 10 minutes. Just before serving, sprinkle over the nuts, then turn off the heat.

Special Occasions

HARLEQUIN KEBABS

These tasty minced-lamb kebabs make an impressive meal for a special occasion.

This is what you do:

Ingredients — serves 4		
I	small onion	I
500 g	minced lamb	I lb
25 g	wholemeal breadcrumbs	I oz
2.5 ml	ground cinnamon	½ teaspoon
2.5 ml	ground cumin	½ teaspoon
I	egg	I
	salt and freshly ground pepper	
12	medium mushrooms	12
I	small red pepper	I
I	small green pepper	I
30 ml	oil	2 tablespoons
2.5 ml	light-brown soft sugar	½ teaspoon

Equipment you will need:
Chopping board, knife, large mixing bowl, kebab skewers, small bowl, spoon, pastry brush, tongs.

1 Peel and chop the onion very finely and put it into the bowl with the lamb, breadcrumbs, cinnamon, cumin and egg and season with salt and pepper.
2 With wet hands, divide the mixture into 20 and roll each mound into a ball.
3 Wash and trim the mushrooms. Cut the top off each pepper, remove the core and seeds then cut the peppers into chunks.
4 Thread the lamb balls onto skewers alternately with the mushrooms and peppers.
5 Heat the grill to high. Place the kebabs on the grill rack. In the small bowl mix the oil and sugar together then brush over the kebabs.
6 Grill the kebabs for about 10 minutes, turning them using tongs, and brushing them occasionally with the oil and sugar.
7 When the kebabs are browned and cooked through, turn off the grill and serve.

Harlequin kebabs and Lemonade

Special Occasions

LEMONADE

Ingredients – serves 6–8

4	lemons	4
125 g	granulated sugar	4 oz
1.2 litres	water	2 pints

Equipment you will need:
Potato peeler, large saucepan with lid, lemon squeezer, sieve.

This is what you do:
1. Wash the lemons then peel off the rind. Put the rind into the saucepan with the sugar and water.
2. Put the saucepan on the stove and heat until the water is boiling. Turn down the heat and simmer for 5 minutes.
3. Turn off the heat, cover the pan and allow the liquid to cool.
4. Squeeze the juice from the lemons then stir into the lemonade. Strain the lemonade into a jug and serve with ice cubes.

BANANA CHOCO MILK-SHAKE

Ingredients – serves 1

1	ripe banana	1
250 ml	chilled milk	8 fl oz
5 ml	Lyle's golden syrup	1 teaspoon
10 ml	drinking chocolate	2 teaspoons

Equipment you will need:
Electric blender

Ask an adult to help you with the blender.
This is what you do:
1. Peel the banana and put into the blender with the rest of the ingredients. Blend until the drink is smooth and slightly frothy. Pour into a glass and serve at once.

CATHERINE WHEEL PIE

Ingredients – serves 4–6

1 kg	cooking apples	2 lb
50 g	raisins or sultanas	2 oz
30 ml	orange juice	2 tablespoons
50 g	light-brown soft sugar	2 oz
200 g	puff pastry, thawed	7 oz
	flour for rolling	
45 ml	caster sugar, plus extra for sprinkling	3 tablespoons

Equipment you will need:
Potato peeler, knife, chopping board, round ovenproof dish, rolling pin, pastry brush.

This is what you do:
1. Heat the oven to Gas Mark 7/220°C/425°F.
2. Peel the apples, then cut them into quarters, remove the cores and slice. Arrange the slices in the dish. Scatter over the raisins or sultanas, orange juice and sugar.
3. On a floured surface, roll out the pastry to a rectangle measuring about 50 × 15 cm (20 × 6 inches). Brush the surface with water then sprinkle over the caster sugar. Starting from a long edge, roll up like a swiss roll then cut into slices about 5 mm (1/4 inch) wide. Lay the slices flat and press them down slightly. Arrange on top of the apples then sprinkle with extra sugar.
4. Bake in the oven for 35–40 minutes or until the top is crisp and golden. Remove from oven and turn off the heat.

Special Occasions

MERINGUES

Ingredients – makes 8		
2	egg whites	2
125 g	caster sugar	4 oz
150 ml	double cream	¼ pint

Equipment you will need:
2 baking trays, non-stick baking parchment, large mixing bowl, whisk, 2 metal spoons, palette knife, wire cooling rack.

This is what you do:

1 Heat the oven to Gas Mark ¼/110°C/225°F. Cover each baking tray with non-stick baking parchment.
2 Put the egg whites into the bowl and whisk until stiff.
3 Gradually whisk in half the sugar, then sprinkle over the rest of the sugar and fold in with a metal spoon.
4 Take a spoonful of the mixture and, with the second spoon, push it onto the tray. Repeat until you have 16 small mounds.
5 Place the trays on the bottom shelves of the oven and bake for 2–3 hours. The meringues should be firm, crisp and still white. If during cooking they begin to brown, leave the oven door open for 2 minutes to cool it.
6 Take out of the oven and turn off the heat. Remove the meringues from the paper and cool on the wire rack.
7 Whip the cream then sandwich the meringues together.

EASTER BISCUITS

Ingredients – makes 12		
125 g	wholemeal plain flour	4 oz
125 g	plain flour, plus extra for rolling	4 oz
2.5 ml	mixed spice	½ teaspoon
125 g	margarine or butter, plus extra for greasing	4 oz
125 g	caster sugar	4 oz
1	lemon	1
1	egg	1
50 g	currants	2 oz
For the glaze:		
1	egg white	1
15 g	caster sugar	½ oz

Equipment you will need:
2 baking trays, 2 large mixing bowls, sieve, wooden spoon, grater, rolling pin, 7.5 cm (3-inch) cutter, pastry brush, palette knife, wire cooling rack.

This is what you do:

1 Heat the oven to Gas Mark 4/180°C/350°F. Grease the baking trays.
2 Put the wholemeal flour into a bowl, sieve the plain flour and spice into it and mix.
3 In the other bowl beat the margarine or butter with the sugar until light and fluffy. Grate the rind from the lemon on the fine side of the grater, and beat into the mixture.
4 Beat in the egg, then stir in the currants and flour.
5 Turn the dough onto a floured surface and knead until smooth. With a floured rolling pin, roll out the dough and cut into rounds with the cutter.
6 Brush the tops with egg white. Sprinkle with caster sugar then, using the palette knife, transfer the biscuits onto the baking trays. Bake in the oven for 15–20 minutes until golden. Take out of the oven, turn off the heat and cool for 1 minute before transferring to a wire rack.

Special Occasions

STARRY BISCUITS

Ingredients – makes about 36

125 g	soft margarine, plus extra for greasing	4 oz
125 g	caster sugar	4 oz
2	egg yolks	2
250 g	plain flour, plus extra for rolling	8 oz
2.5 ml	ground cinnamon	½ teaspoon
125 g	icing sugar	4 oz
10 ml	water	2 teaspoons
1 packet	edible silver balls	1 packet

Equipment you will need:
2–3 baking trays, large and small mixing bowls, wooden spoon, sieve, rolling pin, star-shaped cutter, palette knife, wire cooling rack.

If you would like to hang some of these biscuits on the Christmas tree, make a hole in one point of each biscuit before baking. When cooked and decorated, thread Christmas ribbon through the holes, then hang them.

This is what you do:

1. Heat the oven to Gas Mark 5/190°C/375°F. Grease the baking trays.
2. Put the margarine and sugar into the large mixing bowl and beat with the wooden spoon until creamy. Add the egg yolks and mix again.
3. Sieve the flour and cinnamon into the bowl and mix. Turn onto a floured surface and knead until smooth.
4. With a floured rolling pin, roll out the dough to a thickness of about 5 mm (¼ inch). Stamp out biscuits using the star-shaped cutter then transfer to the baking trays. You will have to cook them in more than one batch. Bake in the oven for 10–12 minutes until golden.
5. Remove from the oven, turn off the heat, and lift onto the wire rack to cool.
6. Sieve the icing sugar into the small bowl and mix to a thick consistency with the water. Spread over the biscuits and place silver balls on the points of each biscuit. Allow the icing to dry before storing the biscuits.

SNOWBALLS

Ingredients – makes 24

375 g	chocolate cake crumbs	12 oz
125 g	unsalted butter	4 oz
15 ml	Lyle's golden syrup	1 tablespoon
30 ml	double cream	2 tablespoons
5 ml	rum essence	1 teaspoon
75 g	desiccated coconut	3 oz

Equipment you will need:
Large and small mixing bowls, small saucepan, wooden spoon, small bowl.

This is what you do:

1. Put the cake crumbs into the large bowl.
2. Put the butter into the saucepan, place on the stove over a low heat and melt. Remove from the stove and turn off the heat.
3. Pour the butter onto the cake crumbs, add the golden syrup, cream and rum essence and stir the mixture. Put in the refrigerator until the mixture feels stiff.
4. Divide into 24, rolling the mixture into balls with your hands. Put the coconut into the small bowl then roll the balls in it until they are coated.

Starry Biscuits and Snowballs

Special Occasions

STRAWBERRY TRIFLE

	Ingredients – serves 6	
8	trifle sponges	8
425 g	can strawberries	15 oz
40 ml	custard powder	2 rounded tablespoons
600 ml	milk	1 pint
30 ml	caster sugar	2 tablespoons
150 ml	natural or strawberry yogurt	5.3 fl oz
	a few fresh strawberries or	
	toasted flaked almonds	

Equipment you will need:
Large glass bowl, chopping
board, knife, can opener,
jug, sieve, medium bowl,
medium saucepan,
wooden spoon.

This recipe can be made at any time of the year using canned strawberries. If you are using fresh strawberries, you can soak the cake with a little apple juice instead of the canned juice.

This is what you do:

1   Cut the trifle sponges in half and put half into the glass bowl.
2   Open the can of strawberries, drain the juice into the jug through the sieve then scatter the fruit over the layer of sponge. Cover with the rest of the sponge then pour over the juice and leave to soak in.
3   Put the custard powder into the medium bowl, pour in a little of the milk and blend together. Pour the rest of the milk into the saucepan, put the pan on the stove and heat until almost boiling.
4   Pour the hot milk onto the blended custard powder then return it all to the pan. Heat again, stirring all the time. When boiling, turn down the heat and simmer for 1–2 minutes until thickened. Stir in the sugar.
5   Turn off the heat, pour the custard into the glass bowl and leave to cool. Cover and chill in the refrigerator for at least 2 hours.
6   To serve, spread the yogurt over the top and decorate with either the fresh strawberries or the toasted flaked almonds.

Special Occasions

REFRIGERATOR CHOCOLATE CAKE

Ingredients – serves 10

175 g	shortcake biscuits	6 oz
75 g	glacé cherries	3 oz
75 g	marshmallows	3 oz
250 g	plain chocolate	8 oz
125 g	unsalted butter	4 oz
2	eggs	2
25 g	caster sugar	1 oz
25 g	icing sugar	1 oz

Equipment you will need:
Chopping board, knife, scissors, large mixing bowl, medium saucepan, medium mixing bowl, whisk, spatula, 23 cm (9-inch) loose-bottomed flan tin, sieve, spoon.

This very rich cake should be reserved for special treats. Cut into thin slices to serve.

This is what you do:

1 Break the biscuits into small pieces. Chop the cherries into small pieces and, using the scissors, cut the marshmallows into small pieces.

2 Place the chocolate and butter in the large bowl and stand it in a saucepan half-filled with water. Place the pan on the stove and bring the water to the boil. When the chocolate and butter have melted, turn off the heat and take the bowl off the pan.

3 Put the eggs into the other bowl with the sugar and whisk until frothy. Pour into the bowl with the chocolate mixture and whisk together until smooth.

4 Stir in the broken biscuits, cherries and marshmallows and mix well. Turn the mixture into the tin, scraping the bowl out with the spatula. Press the mixture down into the tin so that it is level, then refrigerate for at least 2 hours until set.

5 To serve, remove the side of the tin, slide a large knife between the base of the tin and the cake and ease onto a serving plate. Spoon a little icing sugar into the sieve and shake over the cake.

Special Occasions

COBWEB CAKE

Make this marbled cake decorated with a cobweb pattern for Hallowe'en.

Ingredients – serves 8

For the cake:
3	eggs	3
175 g	soft margarine, plus extra for greasing	6 oz
175 g	caster sugar	6 oz
175 g	self-raising flour	6 oz
2.5 ml	baking powder	½ teaspoon
	few drops pink food colouring	

For the icing:
175 g	icing sugar	6 oz
15 ml	water	1 tablespoon
	few drops pink food colouring	

Equipment you will need:
20 cm (8-inch) cake tin, greaseproof paper, scissors, large mixing bowl, wooden spoon, knife, wire cooling rack, sticky tape, sieve, medium bowl, skewer.

This is what you do:

1. Heat the oven to Gas Mark 4/180°C/350°C. Grease the cake tin, cut a circle of greaseproof paper to fit into the base, then grease the paper.
2. Put the eggs, margarine, sugar, flour and baking powder into the bowl and beat together until well blended and smooth.
3. Place half of the mixture in several separate mounds on the base of the tin.
4. Add a few drops of pink food colouring to the rest of the cake mixture and beat until evenly coloured. Spoon into the tin between the mounds of uncoloured mixture, then level the top, leaving a slight dip in the middle. Take a knife and draw it through the mixture a few times to give a marbled effect.
5. Bake in the oven for 40–45 minutes or until risen and golden. Remove from the oven, switch off the heat, then turn the cake out onto the wire cooling rack. Peel off the paper and leave to cool.
6. To make a small piping bag, take a square of greaseproof paper, fold it over to make a triangle; with the long side towards you, take one point and turn it in to meet the top point of the triangle. Now wrap the other point over to form a cone. Stick it together with sticky tape and snip a tiny little bit off the end to make a small hole.
7. To make the icing, sieve the icing sugar into a bowl and blend in the water until the icing is thick and smooth. Spread all but 15 ml (1 tablespoon) over the top of the cake. Add a few drops of the food colouring to colour the remaining icing pink, and spoon into the piping bag. Carefully pipe circles on top of the cake starting from the centre. Now take the skewer and, starting from the centre, draw lines in and out of the circles to make a web effect. Leave the icing to set.

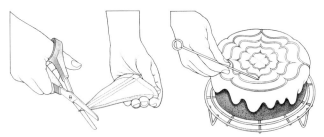

Cobweb Cake

TO MAKE AND GIVE

MARZIPAN WHIRLS

These sweets are particularly nice to make and give at Christmas.

Ingredients – makes 24

250 g	marzipan	8 oz

few drops red food colouring
few drops green food colouring
icing sugar for rolling

Equipment you will need:
Knife, rolling pin,
paper sweet cases.

This is what you do:

1 Divide the marzipan into three equal pieces.
2 Take one piece and add some red food colouring and knead until it becomes evenly coloured.
3 Take a second piece and do the same with some green food colouring.
4 Sprinkle some icing sugar onto the work surface and roll out each piece of marzipan to a rectangle measuring about 10 × 45 cm (4 × 18 inches).
5 Layer up the three pieces of marzipan, lifting them carefully with the help of the rolling pin.
6 From the long side, carefully roll up the stack like a swiss roll, pinching in the end edge. Cut the roll into 1.5 cm (¾-inch) pieces, then put into paper sweet cases.

PEPPERMINT CREAMS

These are very easy sweets to make. The number you have will depend on how thinly you roll the fondant and the size of your cutter. Place them in layers in pretty home-made boxes, to give as gifts.

Ingredients – makes about 60

500 g	icing sugar,	1 lb
	plus extra for rolling	
1	egg white	1
5 ml	lemon juice	1 teaspoon

few drops green food colouring
few drops peppermint essence

Equipment you will need:
Sieve, large mixing bowl,
wooden spoon, rolling pin,
small star cutter, small palette
knife, 2 trays, non-stick paper.

This is what you do:

1 Sieve the icing sugar into the bowl. Add the egg white, the lemon juice, green food colouring and the peppermint essence.
2 Work the ingredients together with the wooden spoon, then gather the mixture up in your hand and knead it on the work surface, dusted with icing sugar, until smooth.
3 With the rolling pin dusted with icing sugar roll out to a thickness of about 5 mm (¼ inch).
4 Using a small star cutter, cut out the sweets, transferring them with the palette knife onto the trays covered with non-stick paper. Gather up the trimmings, knead again and re-roll to cut more peppermint creams.
5 Leave the sweets overnight to dry, then pack into boxes.

Marzipan Whirls, Peppermint Creams, and Chocolate Truffles

To make and Give

CHOCOLATE TRUFFLES

A home-made sweet, favourite with young and old alike.
This is what you do:

Ingredients – makes about 30

175 g	plain chocolate	6 oz
50 g	unsalted butter	2 oz
1	orange	1
75 g	icing sugar	3 oz
50 g	ground almonds	2 oz
	chocolate sugar strands	
	or cocoa	

Equipment you will need:
Medium saucepan, large mixing bowl, grater, lemon squeezer, sieve, wooden spoon, teaspoon, paper sweet cases.

1 Half-fill the saucepan with water. Put it on the stove and bring to the boil. Lower the heat, until the water is simmering. Put the chocolate and butter into the bowl, then place the bowl over the pan of simmering water. When the chocolate melts, remove the bowl from the pan and turn off the heat.
2 Grate the rind from the orange on the fine side of the grater, and squeeze the juice. Sieve the icing sugar then add, with the orange rind, 30 ml (2 tablespoons) of the juice and the ground almonds, to the bowl containing the chocolate mixture. Mix well then leave in the refrigerator until the mixture becomes firm.
3 Take heaped teaspoonfuls of the mixture and, in the palms of your hands, form them into balls. Roll each ball in the chocolate sugar strands or in the sieved cocoa. Place the truffles in the paper cases and leave to set in the refrigerator.

DATE AND WALNUT BALLS

Make these sweets as a pleasant surprise for someone's birthday or for your own party.
This is what you do:

Ingredients – makes 20

125 g	chopped dates	4 oz
125 g	walnut pieces	4 oz
50 g	light-brown soft sugar	2 oz
25 g	drinking chocolate	1 oz
50 g	unsalted butter	2 oz
	icing sugar, for coating	

Equipment you will need:
Chopping board, knife, bowl, small saucepan, paper sweet cases.

1 Chop the dates and walnuts into very small pieces, put into the mixing bowl with the sugar and drinking chocolate.
2 Put the butter in a small saucepan, place on the stove and melt over a low heat. Turn off the heat and pour the butter onto the other ingredients in the bowl.
3 Mix well, then leave in the refrigerator until the mixture feels stiff.
4 Sprinkle some icing sugar onto a plate. Take heaped teaspoonful of the mixture and form into balls in your hands. Roll the balls in the icing sugar then put into the paper cases.

To Make and Give

Ingredients — makes 48 pieces

oil for greasing	
plain chocolate	4 oz
unsalted butter	4 oz
icing sugar	1 lb
strong coffee	2 tablespoons

Equipment you will need:
18 cm (7-inch) shallow square tin, large mixing bowl, medium saucepan, wooden spoon, sieve, knife.

LIGHTNING FUDGE

A very easy sweet for younger children to make but guaranteed to be enjoyed by all ages. For a special treat, add some raisins, chopped nuts or glacé cherries.

This is what you do:

1 Lightly oil the square tin. Break up the chocolate and put into the bowl with the butter.

2 Half-fill the pan with water, put on the stove and bring to the boil. Lower the heat, until the water is simmering. Place the bowl in the pan of simmering water.

3 When the chocolate and butter have melted, remove the bowl from the pan, and turn off the heat. Using the wooden spoon beat the chocolate and butter together until smooth.

4 Sift the icing sugar then add, with the coffee, to the bowl and beat again until smooth.

5 Turn the mixture into the prepared tin, level with a knife and leave to cool.

6 Place in the refrigerator and allow to set before cutting into squares.

To make and Give

Ingredients — makes 6–8

500 g	granulated sugar	1 lb
50 g	butter or margarine	2 oz
10 ml	malt vinegar	2 teaspoons
30 ml	Lyle's golden syrup	2 tablespoons
150 ml	water	¼ pint
6–8	dessert apples	6–8

Equipment you will need:
Large heavy saucepan, sugar thermometer (if available) or cup, 6–8 wooden sticks, non-stick baking parchment, metal tray.

Ingredients — makes about 16–20 pieces

	oil, butter or margarine for greasing	
10 ml	bicarbonate of soda	2 teaspoons
125 g	Lyle's golden syrup	4 oz
250 g	demerara sugar	8 oz
	few drops vanilla essence	
30 ml	water	2 tablespoons
5 ml	malt vinegar	1 teaspoon

Equipment you will need:
Sieve, large saucepan, wooden spoon, sugar thermometer (if available) or cup, 18 cm (7-inch) square cake tin, knife.

TOFFEE APPLES

This is what you do:

1 Put all the ingredients except the apples into the pan and heat over a medium flame until the sugar dissolves.
2 Bring to the boil and simmer for about 30 minutes until the temperature reaches 143°C (290°F), called the soft-crack stage. To test the toffee, if you don't have a thermometer, drop a little into a cup of cold water: the toffee will separate into hard threads if it is ready. Remove from the stove and turn off the heat.
3 While the toffee is cooking, wipe the apples and insert the sticks. Cover a tray with a piece of non-stick baking parchment.
4 Dip each apple in the toffee, twirl around to allow the excess to drip off then place (stick pointing upwards) on the tray to set hard.

HONEYCOMB

This is what you do:

1 Grease the sides and base of the cake tin.
2 Sieve the bicarbonate of soda onto a plate.
3 Put the syrup, sugar, vanilla essence, water and vinegar into the saucepan, place the pan on the stove and heat gently until it boils, stirring until the sugar dissolves.
4 Place the sugar thermometer in the pan and boil the mixture without stirring for about 5–8 minutes or until the temperature reaches 143°C (290°F) (see above).
5 Remove the pan from the stove, turn off the heat, and stir the bicarbonate of soda into the mixture. The mixture will bubble up to the top of the pan. Allow it to cool until the bubbles have gone down a little, then pour it into the tin. Leave to cool for about 10 minutes then use a knife to mark out into pieces.
6 When cold, tip out of the tin and break into pieces.

To make and Give

	Ingredients	
250 g	sultanas	8 oz
250 g	raisins	8 oz
250 g	currants	8 oz
125 g	chopped mixed peel	4 oz
50 g	glacé cherries	2 oz
125 g	blanched almonds	4 oz
1	lemon	1
1	orange	1
75 g	vegetable suet	3 oz
2	medium cooking apples	2
250 g	dark-brown soft sugar	8 oz
5 ml	ground cinnamon	1 teaspoon
2.5 ml	grated nutmeg	½ teaspoon
2.5 ml	ground ginger	½ teaspoon
150 ml	brandy or apple juice	¼ pint

Equipment you will need: Large mixing bowl, chopping board, knife, grater, wooden spoon, potato peeler. Also, you'll need jam jars, greaseproof paper, scissors, material or gift paper, elastic bands, labels.

MINCEMEAT

You will have to ask an adult to give you the brandy for this recipe, or you could use apple juice. Spoon into jam jars decorated with pretty covers and labels to give as presents.

This is what you do:

1 Put the sultanas, raisins, currants and mixed peel into the mixing bowl.
2 Cut the cherries into small pieces, chop up the almonds and add both to the bowl.
3 Finely grate the rind from the lemon and orange and add to the fruit. Stir in the suet.
4 Peel and coarsely grate the apples then add to the bowl.
5 Stir in the sugar, spices and brandy or apple juice and give the mixture a good stir.
6 Spoon the mincemeat into clean jars, pressing it down with the spoon.
7 Cut out small circles of greaseproof paper to fit on top, then cover with circles of pretty material or gift paper and secure with elastic bands. Write labels and stick them onto the jars.

mincemeat

To make and Give

CHERRY CHOCOLATES

These sweets are suitable for very young children to make.

Ingredients – makes 20

125 g	white chocolate	4 oz
75 g	mixed glacé fruits	3 oz
	different coloured cherries, or mixed glacé fruits	

Equipment you will need:
Saucepan, mixing bowl, tray, non-stick baking parchment, teaspoons.

This is what you do:

1 Half-fill the saucepan with water and place on the stove. Bring to the boil then lower the heat until the water is simmering. Break up the chocolate into the bowl and place over the pan of simmering water.
2 Chop up the cherries.
3 When the chocolate has melted, remove from the pan, and turn off the heat.
4 Put a piece of non-stick baking parchment on a tray, then drop teaspoonfuls of the melted chocolate onto the paper. Immediately take about a teaspoonful of the chopped glacé fruit and place it in the centre of each chocolate drop.
5 Leave in a cool place to set, then peel off the baking parchment. Then you can put the chocolates in a pretty box to give as a present, or store in a plastic container.

COCONUT CLUSTERS

Ingredients – makes 24

75 g	desiccated coconut	3 oz
125 g	milk chocolate drops	4 oz
25 g	unsalted butter	1 oz
30 ml	double cream	2 tablespoons

Equipment you will need:
Foil, saucepan, mixing bowl, wooden spoon, paper sweet cases.

This is what you do:

1 Line the grill rack with foil, then evenly scatter over the coconut. Heat the grill to medium, then toast the coconut until lightly browned. Keep a check on it, as it can burn very quickly.
2 Remove the coconut from the grill and turn off the heat. Put the coconut on one side to cool.
3 Half-fill a saucepan with water and place on the stove. Bring to the boil, then lower the heat until the water is simmering. Put the chocolate drops in a bowl and place in the pan of simmering water until the chocolate melts. Remove the bowl from the pan and turn off the heat.
4 Stir the butter and cream into the melted chocolate and, when the butter has melted, stir in the coconut. Drop teaspoons of the mixture into the paper cases, then leave in a cool place to set.

To Make and Give

Ingredients – makes about 27

125 g	Lyle's golden syrup	4 oz
125 g	margarine, plus extra for greasing	4 oz
125 g	soft brown sugar	4 oz
500 g	plain flour, plus extra for rolling	1 lb
10 ml	ground ginger	2 teaspoons
10 ml	bicarbonate of soda	2 teaspoons
1	egg, beaten	1
125 g	currants	4 oz
4	glacé cherries	4

Equipment you will need:
Medium saucepan, sieve, large mixing bowl, wooden spoon, cling film, 3 baking trays, rolling pin, gingerbread people cutters, palette knife or fish slice, wire cooling rack.

GINGERBREAD PEOPLE

You could give these biscuits out at the end of a party for your guests to take home.

This is what you do:

1. Put the syrup, margarine and sugar into the saucepan and place it on the stove. Heat gently until the margarine has melted. Turn off the heat and allow the mixture to cool to room temperature.
2. Sieve the flour, ginger and bicarbonate of soda into a large mixing bowl and pour in the syrup mixture and beaten egg. Mix with a wooden spoon until it becomes a smooth ball. Wrap the dough in cling film and refrigerate for 30 minutes.
3. Turn the oven on to Gas Mark 3/160°C/325°F and grease the baking trays.
4. Roll out the dough on a floured surface and cut out gingerbread people. Carefully transfer them to the baking trays using a palette knife or fish slice and decorate with currants for eyes and buttons. Cut the glacé cherries into crescents, and use for mouths. Gather up the remaining dough, knead and re-roll to cut out further biscuits. Place the trays in the oven and cook for 8–10 minutes.
5. Remove from the oven and turn off the heat. Allow the biscuits to cool a minute before transferring to the cooling rack.

Index

Anzac biscuits 26
Apricot and raisin buns 32

Baked apples 53
Banana choco milk-shake 62
Banana crunch flan 44
Biscuits
    anzac 26
    chocolate chip cookies 38
    Easter 63
    fruit and nut cookies 30
    lemon shorties 36
    peanut butter 32
    starry 64
    tollhouse cookies 29
Boston baked beans 15
Brazilian beef 59
Brownies 33
Butterfly cakes 40

Cakes
    butterfly 40
    cherry almond rock 36
    eccles 34
    refrigerator chocolate 67
    tutti frutti 26
Catherine wheel pie 62
Cherry almond rock cakes 36
Cherry chocolates 78
Chicken
    chinese wings 59
    sâté with peanut sauce 58
    tropical 25
Chocolate chip cookies 38
Chocolate crunchies 28
Chocolate fondue 54
Chocolate muesli fingers 34
Chocolate truffles 72
Cobweb cake 68
Coconut bars 33
Coconut clusters 78
Cucumber dip 8

Date and walnut balls 72
Drop scones 41

Easter biscuits 63
Eccles cakes 34
Eve's pudding 53

Flapjacks, marmalade 37
Frankfurter pizzas 21
Fresh fruit salad 54
Fruit and nut cookies 30
Fruit kebabs 42
Fruit scones 37
Fudge, lightning 73

Gingerbread people 79
Grilled ham with peaches 14

Ham and egg toasties 12
Harlequin kebabs 60
Honeycomb 74

Jam buttons 38

Kebabs
    fruit 42
    harlequin 60

Lemonade 62
Lemon shorties 36
Lightning fudge 73

Macaroni mince layer 20
Marmalade flapjacks 37
Marzipan whirls 70
Melting moments 29
Meringues 63
Mexican rice 24
Mincemeat 76

Oat and cherry squares 30
Orange chocolate mousse 49
Oriental fish fingers 14

Pancakes with butterscotch sauce 46
Peach crisp 52
Peanut butter biscuits 32
Peppermint creams 70
Pizza
    . frankfurter 21
    pie 22

Refrigerator chocolate cake 67
Rice pudding crackle 49

Salad
    fresh fruit 54
    summer 24
    Vesuvius 18
Sardine puffs 8
Sausage pasta pot 16
Sausages with barbecue sauce 15
Scones
    drop 41
    fruit 37
Snowballs 64
Spicy spare ribs 56
Starry biscuits 64
Steamed syrup sponge 48
Strawberry macaroon tarts 28
Strawberry trifle 66
Stripy blancmange 50
Stuffed tomatoes 10
Summer salad 24
Sweet and sour pork 11

Toffee apples 74
Toffee toast 52
Tollhouse cookies 29
Treacle tart 45
Tropical chicken 25
Tunaburgers 16
Tutti frutti cake 26

Vesuvius salad 18